YOUR DADDY DID NOT DIE

YOUR DADDY DID NOT DIE

by

Daniel A. Poling

NEW YORK
GREENBERG : PUBLISHER

922.573

Pシ5y

*This book has been manufactured in
accordance with the regulations of the
War Production Board*

20380

Apr. '45

TO BETTY

Mother of Corky and Susan

Wife of Chaplain Clark Vandersall Poling

AUTHOR'S FOREWORD

This is an intimate story written first for a little boy, Corky, to whom the grandfather is introducing the little boy's "My Daddy." But it has been completed for the little boy and his sister Susan, who was born "afterwards."

One February day in London when I received word that "missing in action" must now be changed to "lost in action," I began a letter to Corky, thinking to tell him of the father whom he would hardly remember. The letter has grown to these proportions, and with the hope that it may have a message for other Corkys and Susans and for other "Pretty Mummie Bettys," I have allowed my letter to become a book.

MOTHERHOOD

Ah, lad with eyes of deepest brown
Uplifted to your mother's face,
With arms that draw the dear head down:
The smile that lights this blessed place,
You rest a moment from your play
And nestle quiet on her breast;
Your ruby lips, what would they say
If they could tell your boy heart's quest?

Oh, lad so cradled in her arms,
Lost to your busy world—intent
To know what stills your child alarms;
This is the boon that Heaven sent.
I, too, have watched her wondrous face
Transfigured when she gave you birth;
Her hand in mine, she came through space—
I saw a glory not of earth.

Ah, Son, this then is motherhood.
My son, this then is motherhood.

Written when Corky's Daddy was three.
James G. McDermid has set these verses to music.

CONTENTS

CONTENTS

YOUR DADDY DID NOT DIE

A LETTER TO CORKY

Dear Corky:

Once upon a time there lived a man named Enoch who never died. What happened to him? Well, this is all that we know about it: "And Enoch walked with God and he was not, for God took him." That, Corky, is written in the Bible about Enoch who never had a funeral nor a grave and who never died.

Now, many years passed and one dark night in the North Atlantic four men stood together on the deck of a ship that had just been torpedoed. Presently her bow rose high in the air and she slid under the water and the men were never seen again. Now these four men are like Enoch, for they had no funeral and they have no grave. But because they, too, had walked with God, we know that God took them. Also we know that they will never die.

For you, Corky, that brave tale of four men who walked with God begins with your "My Daddy."

I first met your daddy on August 7, 1910, in the afternoon. Frankly, he wasn't much to look at and that first meeting came after what was, for me, a hectic experience. You see, he arrived two weeks ahead of schedule. It was like this:

I had gone to a camp meeting near Johnstown, Pennsylvania— they are called "summer conferences," or "assemblies," or "retreats" now—with all my plans made to be at home in Columbus, Ohio, long before the eagerly awaited arrival of your Uncle Daniel's little brother. Oh, yes, we had ordered a brother, but your

3

"*My Daddy*" began mixing his schedules and mine before he wa[s] born, and he certainly kept it up thereafter!

The information that started me on a frantic return trip cam[e] by wire, and what a time I had! In Pittsburgh, with fiftee[n] minutes between trains, I rushed into a telephone booth and afte[r] nearly tearing it down, got my Columbus number. In reply to m[y] wild shout for information as to the condition of a lovely youn[g] mother, I got this, "Congratulations, Mr. Poling, on the saf[e] arrival of your son," and then a professional: "Weight seve[n] pounds, ten ounces. Mother and child doing nicely, thank you.[”] And with that I came to and discovered that I had lost my baggag[e] and was within ten minutes of losing my train! Well, the im[-] maculate stationmaster, who a quarter of a century ago was st[ill] "calling" trains in Pittsburgh, saved me from disaster. I poured m[y] tale into his generous ears; he twisted his handle-bar mustache[s] and said, "Come right along!" Back over my trail we went an[d] there were the bags just inside the gate where I had dropped the[m] as I sprinted through to make my phone call.

I've never forgotten that stationmaster, Corky. Some years lat[er] I introduced your daddy to him when your daddy was just a litt[le] boy. As I was changing trains that August day in 1910, [he] slapped me on the back and said, "Congratulations, son, good lu[ck] to the kid, and God bless his mother." And so not many hou[rs] after the man was born whose name you bear and whom I see [in] your small face, I saw him for the first time. He was lying agai[nst] his mother's breast—nestled in the circle of her arm.

THE SOUND OF MANY FEET

OUR second son grew like the proverbial weed, as fast as a weed, that is, but for the first eighteen months he grew out and round rather than up and tall—in this his wiry son Corky is different. His mouth was all but lost between his bulging cheeks, and was he ticklish! Whenever you touched him, you opened a gurgle or laugh. His parents were greatly troubled when he passed his fifteenth month without showing the slightest inclination to walk or even stand on his fat feet. Lifted to his feet, he would immediately collapse with a chuckle that became a yell if the offense against his own idea of things were too often repeated. Finally, I took the sad case to the doctor, who cut my story short and said with a superior grin, "That boy has more sense than his father, considerably more; his bones are too soft for his pounds. Give him time. He'll be running your legs off soon enough." And sure enough, in another three months he began to do it! But there was nothing precocious about his babyhood; his older brother took all the ribbons for "firsts"—tooth, walk, talk, everything. However, let it be written here that when he did start, he was certainly on his way. Particularly with his talking did he give his father plenty to think about.

It is a great thing to have two boys in a family, close together—almost as nice as the arrangement with Corky's sister Susan, a year old when he is a veteran of three and a half. Our two (we named them Daniel and Clark—Daniel, the elder, and Clark, his younger brother) were certainly the greatest combination I have experienced or known. In fact, it was a combination that "combined" only in the presence of another combination. Then it was two brothers whose four fists beat as one! Between times—and the between times are the times I know most about—action on the home front was of the quality of all family struggles and of all civil wars. Since Corky's junior is a little girl, I am sure he will know nothing of the former; but in due time he is destined to read about the latter.

For a time Clark was helpless before the superior strength, wisdom, and agility of his elder brother. Everything was against him, but his own fat chiefly, with the inevitable collapse that came when he was tickled. Daniel knew how to tickle before he learned to talk. It was an unfair weapon, very unfair; also very effective. A mean advantage that I hope Corky will never take! And yet the brothers were devoted to each other. Even now I smile as I remember the depth of feeling with which Daniel would say, "*My* leddle Bruder Clark"—there were times, I confess, when he said it with added emotion just after he had pinched the "leddle Bruder" or punched him in the ribs.

When our first daughter was born, jealousy for the first time entered our family circle and, believe it or not, it had to be "diagrammed" for us before we parents recognized it. Mary arrived sooner after Clark than he had followed Daniel. Indeed, she is only eighteen months younger; he was just beginning to stagger around when Mary arrived. But then she was the answer to a child's prayer; and also I was not at a camp meeting when she was born. I was right there! . . .

All our children were "received" at home. No hospital for our family—no siree! We began our home-comings right at the beginning. Indeed, to be born in a hospital in those days wasn't considered good form by a good many people. Then, too, there were stories of babies getting mixed and, of course, we wanted the originals. But confidentially it was a financial reason, rather than an altruistic or moral one or any fear of bringing home the wrong baby, that kept us away from hospitals, if you must know. Our children came into the world more rapidly than salary increases. At that, we did almost get to the hospital before Jane arrived. Really, that was a very distracting experience, for we were poised, as it were, "between two worlds," and with a taxi waiting downstairs. Well, we got back upstairs just in time to meet Baby Jane. Oh yes, and the lights went out and when they came on in just two minutes, Jane was there! It sounds simple enough, but the doctor gave me a baleful look and muttered something about the dumbness of starting too late and then said in a clear voice that "another one like that and I'll preach and let you do the doctoring"; and was my face red— it was as red as the new baby.

. . . But where was I? Oh yes, the arrival of Mary and with her the entrance of jealousy into the family Eden. It was like this. When the new baby was ten days old, I came home from the office one afternoon and found the nurse in wrath and our beautiful mother in bed and in tears. It was the nurse who gave me the particulars. For a week Daniel had been "off the reservation" (a family phrase that at another time I shall explain to Corky). He had pinched and tickled and thumped his small brother every time the nurse turned her back, and always when Clark would waddle up to the cradle (yes, we used a cradle; Corky was "cradled" in a bassinet) to admire his baby sister. Daniel would push him away and the howls that resulted certainly were not speeding the recovery of the young mother. That very afternoon things had come to a terrific climax when Daniel hotly pursued by the irate nurse took a short cut over the small gas stove and—well, there could have been a very serious sequel to that story. And so the nurse said to me, "Mr. Poling, either you straighten that boy out or *I leave*," and then he began to cry. Well, a man's work is never done and then and there I began again.

Daniel's small face was very solemn, his mouth very firm, and his eyes defiant. I began by using my best rhetoric to paint a picture of a grateful family into which had come a baby sister. How happy we were! How eager to have Mother up and about (that was subtle), and now Mother was not doing so well. Why? Because of a boy who was naughty, a small boy who pinched and shoved his brother, disobeyed the kind nurse, over-turned the stove—"Daniel," I said, and I had reached my top form, "Daniel, we prayed for a little sister and God sent us one. God sent you and your brother Clark, and now—"

But that was as far as I got. Daniel had faced me until now with stoical calm. I had not even dented him, but at that last he exploded. Bursting into a torrent of tears, he cried, "No! no! Not his sister, my sister, *all* mine. *I* asked God. He can't talk. He didn't pray. My sister. If he wants a baby sister, let him ask God for one"—and that was that!

Well, we managed the matter somehow and came through another crisis—perhaps our first family "theological" crisis—but Mrs. Livingstone, the nurse, never quite got over the experience. Years later when Clark was in college and Daniel in a theological seminary, I visited her in Columbus, Ohio. She was blind and sat, white-haired and alert, as I answered her questions about "her" children. She saved Daniel for the last, but finally she said, and I detected a trace of hesitation in her voice, "And Daniel?"

"Yes," I replied, "he's in Princeton now—Princeton Theological Seminary."

"Thank God," Mary's old nurse ejaculated, "thank God! I knew that boy would be either a preacher or a convict!"

There were hilarious times while Clark was developing two perfectly sturdy legs. (Long before he could walk on them his brother, to his own advantage, used them as handles.) One late afternoon I found the small kitchen in an uproar. The children's mother had been called by emergency illness to a neighbor's telephone. She was gone less than five minutes, but that was ample time to turn a kitchen upside down. I found the small sister pounding her spoon on her high chair and screaming with delight while her elder brother swung her younger in a wide circle across the greased linoleum. The scamp had taken a full pound of the family's butter supply—and that was the full supply—had greased not only the floor, but also his brother's diapers, and achieved the unholy purpose that I am sure was not born in a minute, though executed in even less time when his mother's back was turned. Daniel was always "fast on the draw" and "quick on the trigger"—perhaps such expressions as these will be quite unknown to the small boy when he is first able to read this long letter, but his daddy's youth knew all about them. . . .

Already you will have discovered that in writing about our younger son many others must be written about. In our lives always we are associated with people; but our son (whose name Clark's mother gave to him and who received it from a very great man whom we came to know and love—Dr. Francis E. Clark, founder of Christian Endeavor) was so completely identified with people, so wrapped up in people, and so greatly loved by people, that he could scarcely be written about at all or even referred to without the sound of many feet mingling with the beat of his. Always he was like that! From the beginning when his wobbly legs carried him to the side of his sister's crib, he was going where babies were; playing gently with little children; sitting thoughtfully with troubled young people and challenging them to climb the guarded heights; interesting himself in juvenile delinquents; and sharing his radiance with underprivileged boys and girls. His friendships honored him and I am sure that every friend of Clark's could write as one has written: "Oh, how he enriched friendship."

He had many friends. But equally interested was he in older people. I have seen him on the lap of one of his grandmothers, stroking her rather ruddy cheeks and smiling up into her eyes. He had a way with women, and when he was older he would stand by that grandmother's chair and softly touch her cheek and say, often to the dear lady's embarrassment, "You are *beautiful, my dear!*" One of his most intimate friends was a distinguished New York banker and patron of the arts, the senior elder in my old New York Church—E. Francis Hyde. It was something to see these two—the prep-school lad and the venerable man of 91—to see and hear them together. They talked of ocean voyages (Mr. Hyde had made nearly a hundred round-trip Atlantic sailings); of the sun's eclipses (Mr. Hyde had followed them over the world); and of music and of books (Mr. Hyde was the founder of the New York Philharmonic, and his library was one of the most diverse and one of the largest in Manhattan). The boy would go to the home of the aged man just off Fifth Avenue on 59th Street, and each would refresh and enrich the other.

Yes, Clark loved and was loved by people, young and old, girls and boys, women and men who now are scattered over the world. Just a little while ago among his papers Betty and I found in mountain climbing togs the picture of a young English lad whom Clark met before the War at a great conference in Oxford. Perhaps we shall never see that young man face to face, but his letters reflect the quality of the friends Clark made.

He was often deeply and "finally" in love! The first time in Port Washington on Long Island, not long after he started to school. Perhaps the young lady's Shetland pony had something to do with that. The names varied and the number grew, but every girl was lovely and whether he was finally "jilted" or whether his own ardor cooled, the friendship that survived was always worthy and fine. Of the "one woman" in his life I shall have much more to say—the woman whom "God gave him," and whom he taught his little son to call "Pretty Mummie Betty."

. . But goodness gracious, where are we now! Oh, yes, in the kitchen with the butter on the floor.

There were many experiences and ordeals for our family similar to that kitchen episode before Daniel and Clark finally squared off each in his own right, competent to look after himself in boyhood's affairs and each eager to do so. They were inseparable, but they could not live long in peace together. Each was an individual; each was argumentative; it took a belligerent third party to make them forget their emotional differences. They were quite a pair when they united on a common objective! Daniel was quicker on his feet and more versatile with his body. Clark had the edge in debate—he never lost a debate; that is, he never acknowledged defeat and when *you* went to sleep *he* was still talking. On one memorable occasion in Hastings-on-Hudson after arguing with his mother far into the night, he stopped abruptly and said, "All right, Mother, you win!" She was so done in that she hadn't strength even to question the unprecedented concession. But the next morning at the breakfast table he greeted her with: "Mother, I've got to be honest with you. You didn't get anywhere with that proposition last night. But I just got so sorry for you I had to let you go to bed—now it's like this . . ." and he was off again!

I tell you he was a trial. You couldn't spank him for talking, especially when he was always rather courteous about it; and anyhow Solomon's warning never applied to one of his temperament—"Spare the rod and spoil the child." Definitely the "rod" did spoil him, though on occasion it accomplished wonders with his brother. Daniel would even come and ask for "it" at least once every six months, and weep in sympathy over the hand that had disciplined him! Believe it or not, so it was. Once Clark said to me in a burst of deep confidence, "Daddy, when I become a father, I'll show you how it should be done. I've been observing.

I wish I could do something to show you right now, but you won't listen to me."

It was apparent that he wanted me to accept his challenge to debate, but I was too busy and so I said, "Listen, man, I have to earn a salary to put coal into your furnace and shoes on your feet, and you'd keep me here talking until next Christmas."

At that he shook his head with a dry grin and said, "Well, it might be worth your while—you'd learn a lot!"

I am glad there were other times when I heard him through, or at least listened until he had to excuse himself and go to the bathroom. For he always reacted like that to his own oratory and he had the family weakness that we generally outgrow before we are twelve. (Corky doesn't need to worry; at three and a half he has broken all family records. But in their time his daddy and granddaddy did—terribly.)

Clark had a sense of humor that got him into some difficulties but that carried him through a good many more, and it began to function quite early. He was as hard to get off to bed at night as his own son has been; one year as the Holiday Season approached, he even lengthened his evening prayers to delay the going. He would begin with great deliberation and indicate surprise and even grief when he felt himself hurried. "Now I lay me down to sleep" was always followed by an extemporaneous prayer in which the immediate family were mentioned by name, beginning with "Dear Lord, bless Mother." Well, ours is a large family, and that year Clark developed a deep interest in and a great memory for uncles and aunts and cousins; also he grew fervent in supplication for the police, firemen, boy and girl playmates—and he introduced many pauses between names. It was really a delicate situation to handle, for he had been taught the significance of prayer and the young rascal knew that he had his parents in a quandary. But finally the end came with a bang when "Santa Claus and Mrs. Santa Claus" were added to his bed-time roster. After that he was instructed to conclude with "and all other loved ones and friends," which, of course, included the Santa Claus family. However, the sorrowful expression on the small boy's face, as with all the speed of a venerable rheumatic he lowered himself to his knees, gave the man who is now a grandfather a guilty pang or two.

One afternoon when he was three, I returned from the office to find him in profound disgrace. He had almost ruined the front bedroom that with a great deal of care and perhaps a bit of skill, acquired the hard way, I had just repainted and repapered. Having been sent upstairs in temporary eclipse, he had walked many times round the room, over the bed and everything else in his way, dragging his colored crayons along the walls after him. The results of his amateur artistic efforts were variegated and appalling. That room had to be redecorated by his father.

He had been sent to bed and there I found him. Hearing my approach, as I came into his room he drew the blanket over his face and held it there firmly while I began the preliminaries. I gave him the full benefit of my very deep feeling—Love's Labor Lost, and all that. What he had done to undo all that I had done to make a beautiful room in our happy home, a room for Mother, who was now broken-hearted. I got myself into a proper state of self-pity and then I ordered: "Clark Poling, look at me—aren't you sorry and ashamed? Look at me right now!" And he obeyed. Slowly the blanket came down until his dark eyes were uncovered. Now we were face to face and then he winked, yes, winked at me, the injured party, winked at me, his father—and what do you suppose I did? Well, just keep on guessing.

It was a few months later in that same year after Clark had celebrated his fourth birthday that it became necessary to remove his tonsils. Back from another trip I came to accompany his mother and him to the private clinic of our doctor. That day will never be forgotten in our house. The small boy had the sense of impending unpleasantness and there was a lengthy discussion before he finally gave a grudging consent to this particular street-car ride. Then when he reached the doctor's office, uncertainty became conviction; and when we came to the white room where he was to be made ready for the operating table, stark terror seized him. He cried and struggled, struck out with his small fists and pleaded to be taken home—all at once. Finally, after everything else had been done, I lifted him in my arms, pinned his arms by his side, and held him for the nurse. Then as suddenly as his violent fear began, he calmed.

Relaxed and submissive, he looked up into my eyes and said, "Daddy, will you stay through?"

I answered, "Yes, son, I'll stay through."

Later in the operating room Dr. Brown said, "You needn't worry now, Mr. Poling. He's asleep and will never know—and this isn't always nice to look at under a complete anesthetic."

I was at the door when I remembered. I turned and said, "No, Doctor, *he* wouldn't know, but I would, and I promised the little fellow."

Perhaps it was an hour later that Clark's black eyes fluttered open and then closed again for a few minutes. Gradually his eyes stayed open. They focused on his mother's face, then on mine, and on mine they stayed. I grinned at him and nodded my head. He smiled a little and tried to speak, tried once and again. I bent over him and then I heard him say—the words gave him a struggle, but he got them out—"Daddy, did you stay through?"

It would have been too bad not to have had the right answer.

We had a grand time with stories when Clark and his brother were little boys; and their sisters, too, enjoyed sitting in on the tales of David and Abram who were of rugged pioneer stock, had "ferocious" adventures, and were never allowed to become interested in girls! I produced these children of my imagination one evening when I was keeping the home fires burning in the ab-

sence of the real head of the house, and for nearly ten years thereafter David and Abram were just about the most important members of our household. We followed their adventures from the
Allegheny Mountains in Pennsylvania, where my mother was
born, down the great valley of Virginia and along all the trails
of Daniel Boone. We went with them into the region of the Ohio
River valley. We followed on their journeys of discovery into the
caves of Kentucky, and we were right at their shoulders when
they found the smoking volcano. Yes, sir! We were there. We
scouted Indians and saved many a wagon train. However, when
we rescued two lovely young maidens—twin sisters—Clark let
out a howl, joined immediately by Daniel. "Now they're going to
fall in love and get married, and I won't have it!" he said. And
so we didn't, though I am bound to confess that David and Abram
were certainly headed for the altar that night.

No, they never got married—they came to us as little boys of
a log cabin home in western Pennsylvania and we left them
somewhere in Arizona, in the vast silences of the mighty desert,
left them as sturdy lads who were brave and gentle, wise and
faithful, always equal to the tests of their far journeys, true to
God and country, but quite immune to the attractions of girls
and women. As Daniel once expressed it, "You can't fight Indians
and have adventures and have girls around," and Clark added,
"Of course—only you've got to save 'em!" And so David and
Abram saved lots of " 'em" but traveled on immediately. The
"David and Abram" stories ended, I think, when we returned
from our enforced year of vacation in the Southwest, after a
Fourth of July automobile accident in 1921. It was in 1923 that
Daniel went off to prep-school and a year later Clark followed
him, but to another school. (When the away-from-home school
days began, prep-school, college, and seminary found them in
different institutions. Why? Well, because they were different,
very different, Clark and Daniel.) Yes, David and Abram are still

somewhere in Arizona, I guess, but how closely they companioned Corky's father wherever he went, I discovered in the very last letter he wrote me—the letter that was mailed back from Newfoundland.*

There was another family serial that had its origin in Hastings-on-the-Hudson and was more especially for the boys' sisters, since it began after Clark's prep-school days started. It had to do with the earliest inhabitants of the vast country beyond the Palisades that rose into the sunrise or sank into the shadows far beyond the broad plane of the river upon which our high-set house looked down. But "David and Abram" was *the* story. Perhaps when Corky's cousins, Dutch and Danny and Phil and Susan and Nancy and Gretchen, come to "Long House" in New Hampshire, I shall tell them all about it—and now I *am* getting myself into trouble.

Corky prefers "Little Black Sambo" stories, the stories his father told him so happily, so gloriously, and to which he refers in that same letter. Indeed, I have gotten myself into the swing of them, too, and on these overseas war missions which have carried me to Africa, Europe, India, and China, flying nearly a hundred thousand miles, I have thought of Corky and his daddy and looked for "Little Black Samboes" to bring back to the waiting small boy. But, of course, "Little Black Sambo" is Clark's very own. . . . I am just filling in for him.

Perhaps the greatest sensation that Clark and his brother ever produced, one that scented an entire community of New England—and a most respectable community it was—occurred during my overseas absence at the time of the First World War. Though I was not at home to experience the wrath of my neighbors, and though other hands than mine were "laid on" the culprits, the tale was still alive when I returned; and it remains as the classic of its kind in that good town. The brothers found a skunk, or rather

* This letter appears on pp. 131-132, Chapter 7.

what was left of it after the wheels of an automobile had finished
their cruel work. The animal must have been young and vital,
for he remained a long time in the nostrils of those across whose
lawns he was dragged by "those Poling kids." They did their
loathsome work well. Up and down the starlit streets of the town
they traveled, and finally left the remains in the back yard at the
very doorstep of Dr. Amos R. Well, one of my Christian Endeavor associates and my nearest neighbor. Of course, the thing
could not be hid, for certainly it had not been done in a corner,
and the brothers were not hard to find! They were compelled to
cart away and bury their dead. Then their clothes were as deeply
buried, and finally they paid and paid again and yet again for
their sin. Daniel still generously shoulders the principal blame
for the offense, but Clark with typical spirit tried to argue him out
of it.

In the same lovely village occurred one of the memorable ex-
cursions of all my days with Clark and his brother. It was the
morning of Thursday, October 12, 1916, and Boston—famous
for a hundred shrines of American history and distinguished as
one of the greatest educational, literary, and musical centers of
the New World—on that day was stark mad with baseball
enthusiasm.

The Red Sox on the preceding day had soundly trounced the
Brooklyn Trolley-Dodgers in the fourth game of the World Series.
All fandom—and that means pretty nearly all the inhabitants of
the United States and Canada—was breathing in short staccato
gasps, waiting for the umpire to announce the rival batteries for
the last game.

The day was flawless—an open sky without a cloud, air crisp
without being sharp, and a sun that gave every blushing leaf an
added tinge of gold.

I sat in my office busied with some of the extras that would not
respect even a holiday. With unusual deliberation I signed my

letters; and finally, with the small tasks all done, I settled back for a finish fight with myself.

I wanted to see that game. Every passing moment added to my desire and increased the fever in my blood. But it was a holiday, a day when the feet of children do not tramp the corridors of schoolhouses; and this particular holiday was the first of the year with chestnuts on the ground.

I knew that two small boys and their wee sister were waiting in the hall at home for the telephone bell to ring and for a man's voice to say: "Hello there; get your sweaters on; have the buckets ready. I'll be out on the one-o'clock."

And then the telephone took my attention. An impatient man yelled in my ear: "Hey, you! Do you want this ticket? There are seventeen thousand insane men and boys trying to take it away from me. Speak quick, or I'll be assassinated."

It was my friend talking, and he was holding a place for me in that baseball park to the last moment.

But the fight was all over; I said in a voice of sublime hypocrisy, "Sorry, old chap, but I have an important engagement. Many thanks. I'll do as much for you another time."

I made the one-o'clock after edging through the crowds bound for Braves' Field. Trying to feel cheerful, I found a seat. The car was not crowded going out! At the Back Bay an old man came in and with a cry of amazement dropped down by my side. After carefully adjusting his glasses, he sized me up; then he said with fine scorn: "Well, I thought that every man on the verdant side of seventy and not under legal restraint was on his way to the ball game. You are not seventy, and you don't look like an escaped inmate."

"Your diagnosis is correct and complimentary," I said, "but I am going chestnutting with my boys."

The old man dropped his jester tone, lost the banter from his eye, and said brusquely, "Sir, I would give a million dollars for the chance to go chestnutting with *my* boys. I used to dream of that sort of thing—but the boys never came."

We sat in an understanding silence for the twenty minutes that elapsed before the conductor shouted "Newton" and the old man dropped off.

There was length to my stride and a spring in my step when I turned into my own street; and with the indescribable thrill that a man never knows until the fingers of his little ones rest convulsively in his hands, I greeted the children as they came shouting to meet me. Such a bedlam of voices! No chance for a single minute of postponement. Without changing a thread I was off to the woods.

What an afternoon it was! I lost my fountain pen; I accumulated a larger stock of thistle burrs than of chestnuts; a club from the hands of Daniel, on its return trip from the upper branches of a tree, contributed a lump on the top of my head to the miscellaneous collection of the day.

Coming home, the "little lady" lost one of her shoes, and with a tearful intercession beguiled me into carrying her. We were late for supper, and I was too tired to eat any of it. The children were sure they had had a glorious time. The dining room sounded like a circus tent, and with each voice crowding in on the others the three told their mother all about the great adventure.

Any regrets that might have troubled me earlier in the day were all forgotten when Clark, hugging me about the knees, said in a sudden burst of confidence, "Daddy's all right, Mother; feel the lump on his head."

In the morning a friend with malicious enthusiasm gave me an illuminated description of the game I had missed, and the only one I could have seen. But he was disappointed. My lack of remorse was too evidently unaffected and too genuinely sincere as I said, "Well, I went chestnutting with the children. Feel the lump on my head!"

When I went to France in the First World War, I left Clark, his brother Daniel, his sister Mary, and his baby sister Jane—who was just five months old—with their mother in an old white house in Auburndale, Massachusetts. We did not know that our "Little Mother" (for whom Corky's sister Susan is named) was even then seriously ill; but she was very, very ill. She never told me of her suffering, so that I did not know how cruel was the pain that my going caused her. My sister Mabel—Clark loved her as another Mother; so did his brother and sisters—came from far-off Oregon to help the little Mother.

Most wonderful became the ministry of this young Oregon girl in that white house of growing anxiety. (Some day Corky shall know more about his grandmother who died just after I came back from France, more than twenty years before he was born.) She was very beautiful in face and form and spirit. She came from a great house on an Ohio farm and from a family that has given much to religion and life. She loved all of us with every strength of her radiant being and though her children were all too young to really know her, she lives in each of them like a song that never ceases or a fragrance that never dies. Clark even as a little boy was very loyal to her memory and tried so hard to keep it clear and strong. After he was in college he wrote a poem about this lovely mother of his—a poem that a very great man, William Lyon Phelps, said was one of the student productions of its year.

LITTLE MOTHER

Here, my mother,
"Pretty Head,"
Is a rose
A deep dark red.
You are white.

Look, dear Mother,
At the cloud,
It would make
A ghostly shroud
Soft and white.

Gentle Mother,
May I ask
Why your face
Is like a mask,
Still and white?

Little Mother,
Have you heard
The new song
Of mocking bird?
Why so white?

See, my mother,
The blue sky
Where the birds
Fly silent by.
Oh, you're white!

Dearest Mother,
Can't you hear,
Don't you see
That I am near?
You're so white.

Oh! My mother,
You are dead;
Lying there

Upon your bed,
Cold and white!

Mother! Mother!
Lift your head;
Rise again
From your bed,
White, all white.

Gently falling
Comes the snow;
All is still,
The clouds are low,
Cold and white.

Weeping, weeping,
Soft I tread
On the snow
By Mother's bed,
Cold and white.

Those were very sad days for all of us, after Clark's mother died, and it was Aunt Mabel who brought the sunshine to our darkness. She gave so much to each of us—so much of herself that never shall we be able to thank her adequately. All that our "Little Mother" would have wanted to have done, Aunt Mabel seemed to know about, to understand; and these things she did unsparingly.

After a time a very wonderful thing happened to our family, more wonderful than ever a mind could think or my pen could write. God sent a second mother to us, and I am sure that only Clark has ever put into language just what she became to him and to all of us. Corky's mother and I were looking through

Clark's papers one evening when Corky was fast asleep in a room upstairs, and we found these verses neither of us had ever seen before:

MY SECOND MOTHER

At your feet, my Second Mother,
    This poor heart of mine I lay;
And the years will bring no other
    Dearer than you are today.

For in years of happy living,
    Since you came to mother me,
Always have I found you giving
    Strength and love unstintingly.

Clark's second mother knew and loved his first mother, and it was kind of God to heal two broken homes and from two broken families to make a united house. Never in the world has there been a more blessed union. Clark and Daniel found themselves with two new sisters, dark-eyed little Rachel and Ann— sisters who had always wanted brothers! And Rachel and Ann, who could scarcely remember their own splendid father, had now another daddy. And six little children within the love of a glorious woman came to think of themselves as doubly blessed and richer than all other children they knew, since they had also a mother and father in Heaven.

When "Billie"—Treva Mabel—was born, she became the "connecting link" and the darling of the six, and sometimes I think her brother Clark's particular joy and pride. Of her memories of him she has written:

"When I was seven, I must have been an 'ugly duckling.' I had freckles and straight, straw-colored hair and arms and legs too long for the rest of my body. Little wonder it was that when Clark came home to Long House from his first year at prep-school he should say as he looked me over, 'Well, I didn't think anyone could be quite so homely!' Of course, he didn't mean it quite as it sounded to me, but my eager welcome smile was quickly turned to tears and I fled from the room. Then Clark followed and caught me in his arms and said, 'Don't you worry, Billie. I'll love you anyhow, always!' And that is how I remember Corky's daddy, remember my brother in that incident so poignant to me, when he held me in his arms and said: 'Don't you worry . . . I'll love you always!' "

So complete and perfect was the "blend" that even the maid who lived in the bosom of the family for more than five years was quite disgusted with herself because she couldn't unscramble us. The children were always delighted when inquisitive people, trying to invade our sacred precinct, would say: "Well now, of course, the dark ones are *his* and the light ones are *hers*." Very likely the boys would reply, "Oh, yeah?"—which literally translated meant "None of your business." Nor was it any of their business; nor is it ever. Some people who mean well are never happy unless they are fully informed! Well, such people never got any help from Clark and his sisters and brother.

But apparently our house still had a place to be filled. Our mother, whose hands surely were full by this time, nevertheless reached them out to take another. We were in England in 1926— of that wonderful summer I shall write more later—on a brief visit to friends whom our mother came to know during the First World War when she was doing a great work in her native city. There we found Joan, who became Clark's sixth sister.

When Joan was added to the family circle, the brunettes were increased by one, so that now our sisters were equally divided into brunettes and blondes, and "inquiring" friends were more mixed than ever. Generally, they "gave" our mother three and me five,

but what they seemed to miss was the fact that the children themselves gloried that each of us had them all and that all of us had
each other. Clark's "second mother" was responsible for that.

Jane reduced the matter to a conclusion that baffles adequate
appreciation, one that is beyond praise. On another day, when I
had been left alone with the children, I entertained them with
what I tried to make a realistic story of our family antecedents.
I said, "Geographically, we are a very representative family. Your
mother's parents were born in Württemberg near the Falls of the
Rhine and your mother was born in Ohio. Your father's parents
were born, one in Pennsylvania, one in Virginia, and he was born
in Oregon. Five of you were born in Ohio, one was born in Massachusetts, one in New York, and one in England." At that, Jane,
who had been listening with wide eyes and ears, spoke out in her
clear, high voice: "Oh, Daddy, isn't it wonderful how we all got
together!" And so we all feel.

Once Daniel, when he was in Wooster College, spent a
Mother's Day journeying to his first mother's grave, which is in
a lovely country cemetery not far from the house where she was
born. He trimmed the grass and placed the flowers he had brought,
and then sat down where we had turned back the sod and tucked
his little mother under, and wrote a letter to his second mother
who had given him her life, too. I thought that letter was a classic
of its kind and almost the perfection of spiritual discernment.
Only a woman can achieve so great a thing in the life of a boy.
This is the genius reserved to the Mothers of Men.

Ours is an amazing family prep-school and college roster. Never
did two of us graduate from the same college, university, or seminary, though Northfield and Oakwood prep-schools scored doubles.
The grand total is nineteen; it includes Wooster in Ohio, Rensse-
laer Polytechnic, Simmons, the University of Vermont, the University of New York, Columbia, Ursinus, Rutgers, Bucknell, the
University of Pennsylvania, Penn State, Russell Sage, Johns Hop-

kins, Princeton Seminary, and Yale Divinity School. Corky's uncles and aunts did their own choosing, or thought they did, and that is something! Each assembled his or her own catalogues, wrote to registrars, and selected an Alma Mater. Believe me, those were great days for all of us.

Our sons and nearly all of Corky's uncles by marriage were self-help students and worked at everything from mowing Prexy's lawn, hanging wallpaper, and selling bus tickets to washing dishes, waiting on tables, and a little later to serving as student assistants in city churches. During summer vacations there were counselor jobs in camps for children, work on farms and in stores. Clark and Daniel rather upset the social equilibrium in one superior community by going to work in a vegetable garden. Their employer was an Italian who was a kind boss, but that sort of thing just wasn't done, you know. Thereafter other lads became restless in "unproductive idleness." The "Poling kids" had done it again.

The girls did not have the same economic privileges, and so Clark's sisters had the less glamorous tasks at home, but they earned cash, too, and finally with my extra talking and writing and the sublime courage and perfect management from our mother, we all got educated——that is, we all got our degrees.

Corky's uncles by marriage are splendid men who fit in perfectly as sons of the family. One is a university professor, another a busy business man, and the two youngest are in the Navy——one a lieutenant flying great bombers and the very youngest and latest, also a lieutenant, a "skipper" on a submarine chaser in the South Pacific. Corky and Susan have five cousins——Rachel's children, Gretchen and Dutch; Mary's two, Nancy and Philip; and Daniel's one, Daniel Alfred II, whose mother is Corky's one and only aunt by marriage on his father's side.

Perhaps the funniest story of our family repertoire is one that has without conscience been "borrowed," "purloined," or "stolen" by others; but our family knows its true origin. When I was preaching in the Marble Collegiate Church, New York City, we lived for a time in a lower Fifth Avenue apartment, and frequently took the air in a Fifth Avenue bus—Fifth Avenue buses have two decks. On one occasion Billie, the youngest, was seated beside "Ge Ge," our mother's helper, spelling out the signs. On one card a small boy was pictured brushing his teeth with a popular brand of paste. The lad's arm was hinged at the shoulder and bent at the elbow so that the hand holding the brush moved up and down across the teeth with the motion of the bus. "Look, look," Billie cried, "little boy hasn't anywhere to spit!" And she was right. There the little boy was, right out in front of the world, brushing his teeth and with nowhere to spit! I took the trouble to pass the criticism on to the manufacturer and, "believe it or not," within a few weeks a proper bowl appeared on that advertisement and the little boy at last had a place to spit.

And so in those days when Clark was a little boy—a little boy growing rapidly in body and mind—our large family gave him a wide proving ground for his "argumentative proclivities" and for his eager quest of fun and facts.

LONG HOUSE

SOME one has said that it is not where you live but *how* that matters, and of course that is true, but "where" is also interesting and important. Clark lived in many houses and places, for his father was always a "traveling man." We had gone to Columbus, Ohio, so that I could study for my doctor's degree at Ohio State University, and there Daniel was born in a house near the little church I served as a student pastor. Two years later, when Clark arrived, we lived on Miller Avenue on the east side of Columbus, and I was in the first years of Christian Endeavor activities that eventually were to take me over the world.

It was in the Miller Avenue house that Clark's mother contracted whooping cough just before he was born; the doctor said that he was born with the cough! We know now that it was the cough that caused the deep-seated trouble that resulted in the early death of this grandmother Corky never saw. Clark, so little and so very fat, had a terrible time with the cough. We wrapped him from chin to hips with soft bandages over cotton, and when spasms of coughing left him purple in the face, we held him up by his toes until his little throat was cleared of the phlegm. There were times when we feared he would not survive the ordeal. Then, before he was two years old, we moved to another house in Columbus, a small double house on Washington Street where Mary was born.

Let me reassure you on one point; always we paid our rent, though at times in those Ohio days only with great effort and after it was past due. Our moving was caused by a rapidly expanding family, change of office location, and the desire to get the very best for the children with the money we had to spend. The Washington Avenue house was in the midst of good neighbors and next door lived a Roman Catholic family with whom we became fast friends. The head of the house at that time managed the Columbus Senators, the local American Association baseball team (he has become one of the big names in baseball), and his wife was an understanding, lovely person. With children of her own she understood and loved all little children, so that Clark and his brother and these neighbor children had good times together.

On one never-to-be-forgotten occasion Mrs. "Bobby" Quinn demonstrated the "Good Neighbor Policy" that is now a program of international relations, but that thirty years ago was a vivid reality in the backyard affairs of our two little families. When Mary was not yet two weeks old and her mother was still in bed, Daniel eluded the nurse, scrambled through the bathroom window and out on the sloping roof of the kitchen. When discovered, he was directing his unsteady steps back and forth in the tin-lined gutter at the edge of the roof, fifteen feet above a cement walk— he was not yet four, but very ambitious!

Well, it is a wonder that shouting children and excited mothers didn't produce a real tragedy. He was told to get down, to go in, that he was a bad boy, needed a thrashing, and that the policeman was coming to get him. This last produced a derisive shout, for Daniel knew the local "cop." "Let him come," he said, "he can't get up here, he's too fat!" And just what might have happened next is not easy to imagine, for the nurse was trying to get out of the window, and the little mother was ready to leave her bed.

Then came Mrs. Quinn. "Daniel," she said, "you're just wonderful. My, but you're brave! And now you come right in through the window, and I'll take you down to the store and get you a box of candy." And Daniel came in! Right through that window he came, and into the arms of Mrs. Bobby Quinn, nor did she allow the nurse to do any spanking.

"Leave that to his father," she said, "if he still feels like spanking when I get through telling him the story." And down to the store she went with Daniel holding her hand. When later in that same evening I crossed the yard to say "thank you," a little boy, unspanked, still gripped tightly the box of candy an understanding woman who had children of her own had purchased for her neighbors' child. And, of course, Mrs. Quinn had specified that Daniel's younger brother was to share the candy—that was thoughtful and, I am bound to say, necessary.

In Columbus when Clark began to talk, we all attended church services in a small, temporary building whose pastor, Dr. William S. Harpster, was a great youth leader and also my personal friend. His two daughters and one son were always interested in our small children, and with the younger of the girls, Rosetta, Clark fell violently in love when he was a very small boy. She was, I think, always the exception to any general preadolescent indictment he might bring against other members of her sex. She was the ideal of his earliest childhood and the dream woman of his boyhood, and it was his regret that he had been born too late.

Church services in those days were often an embarrassment for me because the pastor frequently insisted that I come to the pulpit and offer the "opening prayer," and that meant leaving two small boys behind with a mother whose arms were full of the small sister. On one occasion Daniel dogged my steps down the aisle and proceeded to put on a gymnastic exhibition before the altar while with closed eyes I tried to lead the congregation in its morning devotions. I was told that the show in front of me got the attention. Clark remained in his seat, but wildly applauded his brother. They both got theirs when we all got home!

We moved from Columbus to Boston when Clark was five,

and during the next four years lived in Brookline and Auburndale.
These were the years in which the War interrupted our family
program, and in 1918 Clark's mother died. Then came a journey
to Wilkinsburg, Pennsylvania, and one year when we made our
home with Clark's grandparents and Aunt Mabel, playing so
heroically the role of mother to four small children. The summer
of 1919 saw us in a cottage at Sagamore Beach on Cape Cod
and later in Boston living in an old house on Revere St., Jamaica
Plain, directly across from the home of a former governor of
Massachusetts, whose entire family became our good friends. But
Jamaica Plain was scarcely ever our home because, though the
house was the first we had ever owned, we left it just before
Christmas and moved to Long Island to be near my work in New
York City.

And now the gracious "Second Mother" came into our lives,
and for the next twenty-two years Clark had her constant care and
love. Our homes in the New York area were many! Two in Port
Washington, one in Kew Gardens, and the white house overlooking the Hudson in Westchester; then several apartments or hotels
in New York not far from Fifth Avenue and 29th Street, where
stands the ancient church I served as pastor or associate pastor for
more than ten years. However, Clark had gone off to prep-school
from the house in Hastings-on-Hudson in Westchester and, save
for visits, knew little of our New York apartment life.

About this time we found in New Hampshire the Long
House that was to remain always thereafter the beloved place
toward which our wandering feet had pointed through all our
traveling days. The purchase of this ancient house—it was built,
a portion of it at least, just after the French and Indian War in
1767—occurred in the winter of 1925, but we spent our first
summer there in 1927, after a vacation abroad in 1926. The unexplored and generally overgrown acreage (the old deed reads "250
acres more or less") revealed, presently, enough good timber to

pay for the place; the garden plot became very productive; and there were small hay fields. Months, yes, years, were spent in restoring the house and barn, but little by little order appeared and a rare colonial warmth and beauty. It was "Our Mother" who was the architect of the interior remodeling, and indeed of the entire project, though generously she awarded me the portico with its white pillars and the "Arizona Room," which once had been the great woodshed. Also she gives me the massive stone fireplace filling the entire south end of the Arizona Room from granite foundation to the roof. That fireplace is perhaps unique among its kind.

Clark loved Long House from his first sight of her, and that first sight was by moonlight and under adverse circumstances, as you shall presently read. Of course, we all loved her, though the love of some was from the first more intense than the love of others; but with Clark it was love at first sight and a sort of mystical union. With his brother and their friends he spent vacations clearing fence rows, getting in wood, working in the gardens, and building the private road over which Corky's small feet already have traveled. No, he was not the best farm hand I have known. He was too often the dreamer and too much the poet to be that, but he loved "every rock on her mountain side and every blade of grass."

He used to brave the laughter of the crowd to describe the "lodge" he intended to build, build out of native granite and logs—a lodge with a dirt floor and for men only, men that *were* men! Later he made some modifications in the original plans; but even when Betty came into his life, it was still a rugged structure on the loneliest, highest point in the township. Indeed, he never seriously considered any woman who was not interested in that lodge and who could not tramp through the wild land to the top of his mountain—tramp, sir, tramp and climb and like it. In that last wonderful summer when Corky was just beginning to trudge about and we were all together, he covered again, almost foot by foot, the ground he knew so much better than any of the rest of us, and he left instructions with Corky's mother concerning the future completion of the long-planned project. Also he had his dream of his son in that picture. Months afterward in a letter he discussed these matters.

I am glad that Daniel and I spent one afternoon struggling across those acres with him. He led us to the spring we had never seen and to the hidden swamp where the small stream rises. He brought us unerringly by a new way to the summit, and then in the twilight we turned home. We razzed him a lot that afternoon; but he took the razzing with a shrug and a grin, for now he was sure of himself. Though I did not know it until months later, already he had interviewed our good neighbor whose colonial ancestors rest in the cemetery which is located in one of our own fields and had taken a verbal option on the "hundred" that adjoins Long House on the south and that completed his project. The crown of that hundred is Wolf Hill, the roof of the township.

That tramp of the three of us was destined to be our last tramp together, the last of the many in New England, Arizona, Oregon, Alaska, Nantucket, on Cape Cod, the Continent, through Essex and Sussex in England, and through the lanes and streets of capitals of the old world and the new. Yes, that long, last tramp through the wild land of Deering in our old New England home is good to remember.

Perhaps the most memorable of all the tramps Clark and I had together—that was not associated with other matters of which I shall write a little later—was our long hike to Mt. Crotchet. After we returned, we studied the route we took that day from Long House and decided we had walked at least twenty-eight miles. We covered distance, kept a swift steady pace, and were back in the mid-afternoon. But we saw many things and talked a lot. We ate our lunch on the summit where the fire lookout stands and we visited the Ranger in the tower. We turned aside to visit some foundations, and I distinctly recollect that the last mile from the Ellsworth place up the long hill and under the power line was done in double quick. Clark stepped out ahead at the last and looking back over his shoulder said: "Tired, Dad! Shall I carry you?" And with that I speeded up and we came home shoulder to shoulder.

Long House takes its name from its length—two great New England houses built end to end. The "new house," erected 150 years ago, first housed a son of the second owner. Each house was complete with kitchen, living rooms, and chambers. Our remodeling has preserved all the old lines, reopened all the old fireplaces, but made of the two houses one house and our home. The woodshed, 53 x 23, we sheathed on the outside, but within— aside from washing down with lye water the wide boards and rough-hewn timbers and adding the floor, the fireplace, and the windows—we left it as it was in the beginning. The adjoining "pig pen" is now a comfortable three-room vacation suite. Leading off to the east is the only room we have added to the ancient structure. This, the ample 40 x 20 study, with its exterior of native pine rubbed to a lustrous brown and its floor of Oregon pine, has a stone fireplace and its shelves are crowded with pictures and mementoes brought from over the world. A somewhat hidden room, it is the gathering place of the Long House Clan when the members meet in their secret sessions—fifteen is the age requirement, sir, but we may change that for the grandchildren! There are twenty rooms in Long House, as well as a glassed-in sitting and dining room porch that is literally among the high apple tree blossoms—and an attic! An attic like the ones Clark's children will someday read about.

From the front of Long House out through the white pillars you may look into the broad face of Mt. Kearsarge forty miles away, and on clear days even without binoculars you may see twice that distance to the white crown of Mt. Washington rising above the Presidential Range. From the lookout on top of the barn you may see even farther. (That barn, as Corky already knows, is filled with wonderful things.) Two miles across the valley is the white house of our "doctor" friend, while three miles away and a thousand feet beneath us you may see, now that the trees have been felled, the village where we trade and where long ago a President of the United States was born. There, too, is the flash of sunlight on the waters of the rushing Contoocook.

About the house are the elm trees we planted when first we came. They have been twice crippled by ice storms and tree doctors gave them up for lost, but they have survived and now give promise of spreading their shade over Corky's children and grandchildren. At the north of the house is a sloping rugged lawn leading down to a tennis or badminton court, a long grape arbor, and a seasonal pond where in winter children love to skate. Our family spent two winters at Long House, and for a dozen years always we returned for the Christmas vacations. Those were golden days! With more than 30° of registered cold weather, we were warm as toast within. The fireplaces were all glowing day and night, but I must confess that steam heat from the huge basement supplied the comfort.

And that basement! I have carried Corky there and often his daddy explored its recesses and pointed out to his friends the granite stones of its walls and fireplace foundations and the small colonial bricks that date these early New England houses. Also he delighted in the wooden shutters that slide into the walls at the front-room windows, the original plaster, and the incredibly wide boards of the "North Stairway."

How firmly Long House stands upon her granite we did not know until the year of the great storm—the great hurricane—which leveled every pine, hemlock, and spruce of the finest stand of conifers in all southern New Hampshire, but left the glorious structure unbroken and unmoved.

We are fortunate in having much of the original furniture in Long House and six generations of family Bibles with their quaintly written family records. There are chairs, a settee, a lovely bookcase, and a meal chest mentioned in a will probated nearly a century and a half ago. (We have a copy of that will!) Even family pictures and ballads the girls of the Revolution sang were left behind, and an old pewter salt cellar and half-burned wicks from the days before Daniel Webster came to take his bride from another white house only twelve miles away. But the small rose-wood piano, one octave short, the first piano in all that region, is the prize piece. It stands where it has stood for a hundred years across the corner of what our mother calls "The Colonial Living Room." Many years ago it was brought up the mountain on an ox-sled from the village as a Christmas present.

Of all the articles found in Long House the maps were the most interesting and, save for one other thing, the most valuable. One of Hillsboro County, printed nearly a hundred years ago, gives in great detail the particulars of Deering Township as of that early time. Every house with the name of its owner and all of the town roads, some of them long since abandoned, are clearly marked. With the map as our guide, Clark, his brother, and I have followed every road and ancient lane and gone to every over-grown foundation. Many are the discoveries we have made and many are the things we have imagined. Another map shows the United States as it was when Lewis and Clark started on their journey. Strange legends fill in the unexplored spaces in the Far West, the West then unknown. The rivers of the Pacific Coast run in all—and generally the wrong—directions. What is today the most valuable farm and grazing land of the continent is marked "Uninhabited." I found that map while looking for a cricket! It (the map!) was tightly rolled and lying between the top of a bookcase and the ceiling of a small dressing room (the case had been moved from its original position). When I flashed my light into the space, I missed the cricket but found the priceless map. The third map is of the original Thirteen States and their territories. Also there is a fourth, not a map perhaps, but pictures done in colors of the time—pictures of the nation's first eight Presidents. I have had all the maps restored and Corky and all the grandchildren will have them to enjoy in Long House days that lie ahead.

Our most valuable tangible possession that came to us with Long House (we would have loved to have the grandfather's clock that for more than a hundred years stood in its corner) is a book. I had seen it many times among the other rather commonplace volumes before I discovered its uniqueness. On the inside of the front cover is pasted a name. By whom or when it was left there, no one knows. The book itself is a hundred years old and describes the "Know Nothing" movement. On its front page it has the watchword "Let only Patriots be on guard tonight" and the picture of Daniel Webster, then the golden-tongued hero of this strange society. The picture is a very handsome steel engraving of the hero. But the name, the original signature pasted on the inside of that cover, is the name of a signer of the Constitution of the United States, the name of a former Ambassador to France, the name of the man who said: "Millions for defense, but not one cent for tribute"—Charles Cotesworth Pinckney! Perhaps some day Corky will write the Long House story about that!

Do you wonder how we learned all that we know about Long House—Long House which Corky and Susan will love as always their daddy loved it? Well, when we first came to live in the old house to which we gave a new name, a great-great-grandson of the second owner, a very old man high in his nineties, for the first few summers came to visit us. He told us about the second of the two houses—the "New House," he called it—which was built before he was born, and about the cherry trees that once lined the road, about barn dances and corn huskings and many other happenings. Then there was a grandmother nearly as old, who had been married by the Squire in our sitting room nearly three-quarters of a century before—married there and by the Squire because the Town Church at the moment was without a minister. Then, too, we had the county history, which gave the historical beginnings of the township and told how it was given the family name of Governor Winthrop's wife—"Deering"— given that name by the good Governor himself.

You see our house once stood in the territory of the old Massachusetts Bay Colony. The road that runs between Long House and the barn follows the earliest Indian trail, and our cemetery was begun where a first settler was found clad in deerskin and dead beneath the tree he had felled as he cleared the ground for his cabin. That ancient burying ground stands on the slope of one of the granite hills of our old New Hampshire farm. It overlooks Deering Pond toward Mt. Crotchet. The crumbling stones are covered with lichen and moss. The mounds are blanketed with wintergreen. It is stony soil, but seed ground not to be despised. Here lie men who fought at Bunker Hill and who marched with Washington.

I go often to this "God's Acre" and stand beside its graves, and I shall take our grandchildren there. I like to breathe the air beneath its pines. I like to feel myself a part of its tradition. Who were these men? Sons of the soil, born of a humble folk who did their duty, they were the commoners of their day. They teach us now a simple lesson: "Do your bit and your best to make the nation that we gave a being—this great and free America—to make and keep it free and great."

This is the lesson that they teach, and with the lesson comes the spirit of the teachers and their faith, faith that human destiny is at last divine, faith that man cannot fail if he is true, and faith that America was not born to die. That was the faith of our son.

Clark went often to that cemetery and took his friends there. We all feel that those whose names appear upon the stones beneath the lichen and moss and whose dust lies under the wintergreen, which in the fall is so beautiful with its red berries, are our own people and that somehow we have become of their breed.

Yes, Clark loved Long House and all her dreams and whispers. He knew that the Arabs believe a dwelling place becomes the residence of the spirits of the departed who have lived within and loved its walls and rooms. He had with his sisters and brothers and their friends, who came from prep-school and college to spend summer and winter vacation days with us, a profound sentiment for everything upon our granite mountain.

We have moving pictures of the cutting of the Long House Christmas trees, of the children carrying them out of the timber and across the fields. How straight and tall those trees stood in the Arizona Room and how straight and tall again they will stand if the children of Long House have their way and we in another Holiday Season can bring it to pass. Surely, never were there times like those—at least within our knowledge and the knowledge, too, of girls and boys, some of them from far off missionary lands, who in their holidays while distant from their own loved ones became as children of our hearts and who felt themselves, I am sure, children of Long House.

How those walls could expand! Never yet have they been overcrowded, though when Rachel married Bill, and again when our mother arranged my surprise birthday party, the timbers must have groaned, but happily! On the wedding night forty-seven men and women, young and old, slept within those walls; and when the lovely bride came to the white altar in the flower-banked Arizona Room, more than a hundred people were there to hear the marriage vows exchanged. A touch of humor—just a touch—was added by Clark's brother Daniel. He had clowned a lot during the preliminaries, and when he stood at last by Bill's side at the beautiful altar, he lost the ring. Yes, lost the ring, for it got tangled in the lining of his pocket and he nearly tore his vest apart before he got it loose! The pause seemed an eternity. Clark's snort of nervous delight didn't help matters any. Later on in the evening he affirmed that the near tragedy was a "judgment of God" upon Daniel for his many sins!

I imagine Corky will be interested as always was his daddy in the tale of Ninean Aiken, who took a platoon of Deering men to join Wolf before Quebec, and who for his services to the Crown received the grant of land of which the present Long House acres were the center. He built or began the first house. But in 1791, so the county history reads, becoming restless and crowded because the township was filling up, he sold his Deering holdings to one Abram Gove and moved west. A few years ago one of his descendants, living then in Texas, came to see the ancient seat of her family.

From 1791 until 1925, Ninean Aiken's Crown grant of land, though from time to time reduced in size, remained in the Gove family. I bought Long House from the heirs of the last of the Goves. They were two sisters, Sarah and Alzira, who had never married. The house, therefore, did not change hands until the name itself had disappeared. That story is a poignant sequel to another. Into the Civil War the town of Deering sent as volunteers nearly all her sons of military age. They kissed their sweethearts good-by and marched off, few of them ever to return, for on that bloodiest day at Vicksburg they were with Hooker's "Stonewall Brigade." The girls of Deering lived on with their memories, but with them died a future that might have been.

Into all of this history and atmosphere, Clark came one moonlit night when with "Tubby" Painter and Kenny Bromage, fresh and very fresh from Oakwood School in Poughkeepsie, he drove up the not yet opened private road. ("Yes, we opened it!" he used to say.) They came to a wild stop at the south door and fairly woke the dead with their shouts. Their car, already a wreck, was now a ruin with its engine block cracked and broken by the rocks in that oxen-sled trail they had straddled but couldn't clear. Nevertheless before the summer was over, they sold the ruin for more than they paid for the wreck and, as one of the trio expressed it, "without the loss of honor." Kenny, the youngest, was covered with baggage when the family came out to greet the noisy arrivals, and our first task was to extract him without breaking any of his small bones. It was just then that I heard our younger son. He looked up at the moon riding high in the heavens —looked at the moon above the wide lines of Long House and said with a voice of ecstasy I shall never forget, "Gee, Daddy, isn't it great!" And great it was and is for all of us, and great it ever shall be.

That first summer and the next were crowded with work; and the road especially became the creation of the boys. Tubby, Clark's prep-school and college friend, became a third son of the house. The Arizona Room was not yet completed and its space was known as "The Boys' Dormitory." It became a veritable chamber of torture for visiting male friends of the older sisters and for other males who might tarry there for a night. The ancient and dishonorable game of "hot-hand," played with shingles, was one of the milder diversions. There were real fights, too; and other stern moments when "men who were men" were determined to prove it. But a grand time was had by all. Daniel always gave the Guernsey cow the name of his girl, and after three summers the poor beast had so many names she responded to none of them. He called her then with carrots.

There are moving pictures of Clark and his friends on the great horses, the Morgans, Ray and Jim, that were half-brothers, and of the little Shetland pony, Nebby, who was wiser than any child who ever rode or drove him. Pictures of the sleds filled with children and with older children, too, and the small black horse trotting through the snow. Also pictures of little girls in a wildly careening cart, for when Nebby was turned toward the barn, he just about broke all the records.

There were affairs for the Boy Scouts in Clark's later years at Long House, for he had a deep affection for the town boys who knew him then and remember him now as their friend. His principal borrowings, and he was generally borrowing or trying to, were to buy wieners for a Scout hike to Crotchet or Monadnock or Kearsarge, or for a roast up by the great rock.

There were always dogs on the farm. In that first year we bought Fluffy, an American shepherd pup—bought her for one dollar. She lived until her seventeenth summer, and every summer after the first until her fifteenth she presented us with sons and daughters—in all exactly 111! She was a beautiful animal; spending her long life in the country out of doors, she had, even in her last winter, the finest coat I have ever seen. She knew and loved each one of us and had a voice of indescribable expressiveness. She was so human that at times she was more than that! For a few years Tarzan, a great Russian wolf hound who gave me walking exercise I have missed ever since his untimely death, was Fluffy's mate, but never her equal. Perhaps presently we shall have another Fluffy for Corky and his cousins. Yes, and another Tarzan, for I have been missing my exercise. But I cannot believe there will ever be another dog the equal of Fluffy.

Save for a few uninvited marauders, there has been just one cat at Long House. We value our birds. But that one cat was a gentleman and a warrior—a Manx cat given to us by one of Clark's uncles. I did not intend to like him, and he knew it. Being of the quality that is challenged by opposition, this homely, yellow little animal with broken tail, short ears, and extra toes, set himself to win me. On his first night at Long House he leaped to my shoulder as I sat at the table and rubbed his cool nose right under my chin, while he purred like an old gentleman with asthma. He took me as easy as that! Ever after, whenever he could, he rode on my shoulder. He would leap to my stirrup as I sat in the saddle, spring from my boot to my arm, and once in position would ride like a veteran. And believe me, he was a veteran! I had argued against taking him because of the dogs, but Clark's uncle laughed and said, "Don't worry about that cat, but take care of the dogs!"

Well, after the first morning I knew what he meant. The Manx, as though fleeing from the dogs' first rush, ran up the trunk of one of the elm trees; then, turning quickly, he dove straight to the neck of the wolf hound. He landed with all the claws of his four feet in action and a scream that sounded like an original fury. Down across the field that great dog went swifter than ever he had gone anywhere before—and he could run. But not until he cleared the wall far below the barn did he shake off his terrible rider. Well, that battle ended the menace of—and to—the dogs. They gave the yellow fury a wide berth and he ignored them entirely.

The Manx came to an untimely death, but an end not unworthy of his spirit. There are wildcats in the ledges of Clark's high mountain, and having vanquished all the foes he could find in the civilized community, the Manx went up to the ledges. He made just two trips. After the first we nursed him back to life and a degree of health. One morning we found him torn and bleeding, left ear now completely missing and a gaping wound in his chest, lying all but dead at the kitchen door. He was given the care his courage deserved and our love for him prompted. Behind the stove he lay for days and only his eyes were alive— they burned with murderous fire.

When at last he was about, we were sure he was cured of his violent passions. I lifted him to my shoulder and he seemed content to doze by a fire. But Clark said, "No, he has a memory, he is a guy that can't forget, and he'll be going back for more. Yes," he insisted, when I expressed another opinion, "your wish is father of your thought, Daddy. You better kiss that cat good-by every night now, for he'll be leaving soon on his last midnight journey." And Clark was right—he went out again and this time he didn't come back.

But the one dog Clark loved, loved so profoundly that afterward he never allowed himself to love any animal so deeply, came into his life before his days at Long House and during our summers in the cottage at Lake Sunapee. A beautiful English sheep dog, "Pal," had been given to the family when Clark was twelve, and Clark it was who came to possess him. Their friendship was a beautiful thing to watch, but its intensity made the early death of Pal a tragedy in the boy's life. The dog became afflicted with shaking palsy and we could find no cure. The beautiful animal was racked by the malady and Clark suffered with his friend. When I took the dog away, the boy went into seclusion. He was silent for days, and indeed never mentioned Pal again; but he carried the picture of the English sheep dog always in his wallet until two years later, when we were returning from our vacation in Alaska, he lost his overcoat and with it the wallet and picture. He valued the coat, and all his money was in the wallet; but when I found him weeping on the rear platform of the train we had taken from Prince Rupert in British Columbia, I knew he was not crying because of a coat or the loss of money.

Oh, yes, there were many other dogs in our family. They are a streamlined procession from the first French bull dog in Columbus, Ohio, to the aristocratic little Scottie who would not get out of the way of an automobile (he despised them) even to save his life. Many dogs there were, but only these about whom I have written were really part of the life of the little boy and young man who became Corky's "My Daddy."

Perhaps the glory of the dogs that are a tradition of Long House is the life they lived in the open. Always I pity dogs in the city—as well as the strong men who direct their ways through city streets. I can understand why some of these distraught animals commit suicide.

Our younger son was part of a very wonderful community in the town of Deering. There were the year-round people with whom he always had so much in common, especially the children. There was the "Summer Colony," doctors and teachers, business men and preachers—young and older—who had many happy times together and many worthy interests in common. Once Clark grinned his characteristic grin and said to the man who is writing this, "Yes, Brother Poling, you picked a good spot to raise a family, and I think I'll pick the same place to raise mine, only—" he concluded and ran "—I have my own ideas and there'll be some improvements!" Now what did he mean by that?

OLD MAN BY THE SEA

CLARK started to school in Auburndale, Massachusetts, and some of his earliest writings had to do with the experiences of those days. One story in particular, which afterward appeared in a college student publication, turned the heat on his brother for certain mental tortures suffered at Daniel's hands. You see, there was a little girl with long flaxen curls who lived just beyond our lawn and who captured Clark's heart and attention. She was a few months his junior. . . .

After Auburndale came Wilkinsburg in Pennsylvania, where the rapidly growing children, mothered by Aunt Mabel, lived with my father and mother in the parsonage of the Evangelical Church.

Clark's son is born to a preaching tradition. His father, three of his uncles, both of his grandfathers, and on his father's side his forbears for seven generations have been, with only one exception among the males, clergymen. Their parishes have ranged from New England to the Pacific Coast, from country parishes to metropolitan congregations; and in the foreign missionary field and editorial sanctum the name Clark gave to his first-born frequently appears. There are many answers to the question "Why?" But one thing I would write here: family pressure was never applied. My father never asked me to be a preacher and I never asked Corky's.

The most exciting episode of the Wilkinsburg days—again there were incidents that brought forth from harassed neighbors the ejaculation "those Poling kids!"—was the finding of a hidden cache of stolen money. Some thousands of dollars were unearthed in the lumber yard and (not without tears) turned over to the authorities. I was in Europe at the time, for after the Armistice I had returned to France with the Y. M. C. A.

Returning from abroad in the spring of 1919, I made my headquarters for a few weeks in Wilkinsburg, Pennsylvania, with the children, their Aunt Mabel, and my parents. That stay was brief, but quite long enough for me to discover how great was my debt to my youngest sister and to my mother and father. Clark, too, never ceased to be grateful for the care and affection showered upon him in that modest devoted home. Years later, in his statement made to the church assembly that ordained him, he said, "Once I lived with a saint . . ." He referred to my mother, his grandmother, who was all that he declared her to be; her life is a story more romantic and beautiful than any I have yet read.

My father, who assisted in Corky's baptism, and whom Corky's daddy came to respect and admire profoundly, in those days faced disciplinary problems that perhaps made him less popular with two small boys. What they didn't think of was hardly thinkable! Clark, for instance, developed the gratuitous habit of keeping his grandfather in order at the table, reminding him of a spoon that might remain in the coffee an instant too long, or of a mature elbow resting on the table; and when I put in my belated appearance, Aunt Mabel was bound to tell me that my second son was a little—just a little—disrespectful. If a crumb or a shred from the shredded wheat clung to my father's unshaven chin, Clark would sing out: "Grandaddy, wipe your chin." Now whatever the motive—and the motive itself I am bound to question—the result was not conducive to family morale.

I took the young man aside at once. I explained fully what I expected in the future and why. He argued, or tried to. Always he could at least try and did. He insisted that his grandfather ought to know when his chin needed wiping, that no one else was thoughtful enough to tell him, and so forth and so on. Well, I finally stopped his perpetual motion by informing him in language not uncertain (accompanied by the promise of suitable action if he failed to give heed) that "a little boy is not the proper person to correct the table manners of, or to give information such as described to, his grandfather." Clark went off, compressing his lips, shaking his head, and, I am afraid, muttering to himself sentiments not yet expressed. However, the last thing that I actually heard him say was: "Well, *somebody* ought to tell Grandaddy to wipe his chin." And to that I replied, "Yes, my son, certainly, but you are not that somebody."

That evening we had apple pie for dessert, and of course it had to happen: a flake, just a flake, the merest crumb of his great-grandmother's unbeatable pie, went its own way and clung to, or shall I say dangled from, his grandfather's chin. Clark's keen eye fixed upon it—no doubt he had been waiting for, looking for, even praying for that very moment. Forgetting our afternoon conference, he raised his hand, pointed his finger, started to speak, and then became suddenly aware of me. He caught my baleful eye fixed upon him, and though he continued to point, with perfect timing, he "changed pace"—that is, he changed the direction of his remarks and said, "Daddy, you tell Grandpa to wipe his chin."

We all came together again at Jamaica Plain, Massachusetts, as I took up with the Christian Endeavor movement my war-interrupted activities. It was from the Jamaica house on Revere Street, just across from good Governor Foss and his lovely lady, that Aunt Mabel left us for her own home in Oregon, and it was there that the gracious presence of the woman of whom Clark has written so poignantly came first to fill our lives. School for Clark in Jamaica Plain was a matter of less than four months, because before Christmas, 1919, we had moved to New York City, and my pulpit, editorial, and organizational activities began, first with the Inter-Church World Movement, then with the Marble Collegiate Church, *Christian Herald*, the J. C. Penney Foundation, and continued with Christian Endeavor. Always Clark was interested in my writing, and before he was in college I had editorial designs upon him. Before I knew of his decision to enter the ministry, I thought of him as a future associate in *Christian Herald*. He was a very early critic of my style and content, and once said with boyish frankness, "If you'd give more time to it and didn't try to do so many other things, you could write!" I was bound to accept the implications.

School days in the New York "theater" were interrupted by half a dozen moves and the long enforced vacation in Arizona, but Clark managed to convince or delude his teachers and so lost no time. I hope that Corky will be the student and scholar of his father's line. Indeed he should be, for he has his mother's inheritance, too. We had to marry our first Phi Beta Kappa key—Clark's sister Billie did that for the family when she captured Corky's Uncle Phil. The only key that Clark ever wore fitted the back door of the dormitory or fraternity house. Ditto for the writer of this story. I am pulling for Corky to imitate his uncle, Lieutenant Philip Roy, skipper of the SC-504, at the moment somewhere in the Southwestern Pacific.

After Arizona there followed one year in the public schools of Hastings-on-Hudson; then Clark spent two semesters at Mt. Hermon, Massachusetts. The headmaster advised against it, for he was very young for so mature a junior college; and the headmaster was right. Was I red in the face when I received a letter from my younger son in which he said, "I am rooming with a fine foreign fellow nineteen years old. I picked him, Daddy. I knew that you would want me to do that." "Foreign fellow"—fine, but the age—not good at all. And so indeed it proved to be, and the next year Clark was in Oakwood, the Quaker school for boys and girls in Poughkeepsie, New York. All my life my children have been "bringing up Father," and now the grandchildren begin to operate.

I have eaten spinach and green vegetables and everything else that you should eat—vicariously. Billie used to wail out with "Daddy, oh Daddy, do you really like it!" I fear that often I lived a lie. But more serious by far were the situations into which Clark sometimes got because he tried to practice what he thought I preached, as for instance in choosing that mature young man for a roommate.

Oakwood days were golden days—perhaps the best days for sheer enjoyment and moral growth of all Clark's days away at school. In Headmaster William Reagan he found a mind and man of scintillating, prophetic quality and a spirit kindred to his own. Oakwood was co-educational, and Clark began then his real life away from home with girls and boys. He found at Oakwood the closest friend of all his school and college days, George "Tubby" Painter, with whom he shared study, athletics, and "family affairs" —Tubby, who came for his vacations to the farm and who became as another son in our family. Oakwood was the student star by which Clark's course was set, and never was its spiritual guidance lost to him. Eventually two of his sisters graduated from Oakwood —Ann and Jane; they, too, were caught by the spiritual generosity and simple dynamic faith of this school and its headmaster.

As to what Clark achieved during his Oakwood days, the letter of a graduate who never saw him is suggestive. "Even then," she writes, "Clark Poling was an Oakwood tradition, and to be your best and finest was to be like him." Headmaster Reagan once said something to me that made me very happy: "Clark has more stuff than his father. . . . He will go farther than his dad!" For that I had only the lame rejoinder: "Well, I picked his mother."

Just a little while ago Headmaster Reagan wrote me a letter in which was this fine word about Corky's father: "Clark Poling was an outstanding personality at Oakwood. He had a high sense of his own responsibility, but he was kindly in his attitude toward the mistakes of others. I remember him above everything else for one experience. My small son had died, and I had returned to the office, just to get acquainted with it again. I thought I could not see anyone that night. When I started home, I found Clark waiting at the office door. I thought I could not discuss school matters with him that night. (He was president of the student body.) He spoke only twice that night. He said, 'I have waited to walk home with you, Mr. Reagan.' When we reached the house, he opened the door and said only, 'Good night, Mr. Reagan.' But what a good night! I could have faced anything after that walk with him. He was not pious, he was fun-loving; one night he rode through the girls' hall in a laundry basket. He was a great tease, but without malice or bitterness, and without any loss of serious purpose."

From Oakwood Clark and Tubby entered Hope College, the "Dutch" school in Holland, Michigan. Our family believes in the small college, the church-directed school, and a very wide family experience confirms the original belief. For undergraduates the small college has in our opinion more of quality to give girls and boys than the larger institution. Then if possible and desired, let there be graduate work in the greatest of the land. Of course, the final decision was always with each son or daughter, and Clark chose Hope. He continued his athletics and also he entered a broad field of reading and writing. From his earliest student years a constant and discriminating reader, now he fairly swept the classics as well as contemporary volumes. I am sure that grades suffered at the expense of extra-curricular activities, but also I am sure as I survey that crowded scene that generally our son chose the "better part." Decisions of this character are always difficult to make, and any decision is bound to contain both profit and loss. I cannot standardize an answer, but if Corky is as fortunate in "what comes out" as was his father, we shall be satisfied. However, I do hope he gets that key, and remembering his mother's blood, I really think he may.

An unfortunate accident in Clark's sophomore year—I shall write of this later—hastened his decision to complete his four years' course at Rutgers University; but Hope was always his college. I believe the future would have found him a vital friend of his Alma Mater. He left behind him there rich and dynamic experiences and Tubby, his other student self; and he carried with him poignant memories and a maturing purpose. Differences that had risen with the faculty over the editorial policies of a student publication with which he was associated never affected his love for Hope, and he was so congenially fair that he gave the faculty the "nod," which was a little more than I could do. May I confess to you that I gave mine to him! Let me add that these differences did not in the slightest influence his decision to take his degree from Rutgers.

Perhaps I should tell now the story of Corky's father as an athlete. He summed it up in the words, "Dad, I'm punk. I can't run and I'm too light and too brittle, yes, I'm punk." From that frank appraisal which was literally correct, he went on to play right-half at Oakwood and to become, in the words of his coach, the best freshman defense back in the Michigan Small College Conference. In those days he never stripped more than 135 pounds, and I never saw him getting into his football togs when he wasn't strapped with adhesive from his shoulder blades down over the old break just below his hip. But there is something more than pounds and speed, and Clark had it—spirit and the will to win. When he tackled or hit the line, he seemed to add an extra fifty pounds to his scant 135, and he didn't stop! His freshman year at Hope was his best year, and save for the opening varsity game in his junior year, it was his last. Hope did not lose a game in his freshman year, and Clark made his sterling contribution not only defensively but as a forward passer and in running the ball.

In that year I saw him in action only once, and though always I feared for his very life, I was very proud that day. Of course Tubby, both at Oakwood and Hope, was a granite wall in front of him—Tubby, who had on any athletic field just about everything. And Tubby it is who says of his friend Clark: "He overcame handicaps by utilizing his indomitable courage and stamina. Also a certain effervescence dominated Clark's personality. This spirit he carried with him constantly and conveyed to his associates. It was this quality that seemed to glow in his eyes and give him the determination to conquer."

That which finally sent Clark off the gridiron and which hastened his decision to go to Rutgers was a fractured wrist—a double fracture. In his second varsity game he passed to a completion for the last time. Never again would he grip a football, and always afterward that wrist, though decreasingly, was a thorn in his flesh. You may think it strange that I did not assert parental authority to keep him out of football, since he was really too light for the game. No, to do that might have broken something even more important than a wrist—had I been able to keep him out.

There are two matters that should be added before we go to Rutgers: a further word about our son as a youthful composer and writer, and a statement of his ordeal with pacifism.

At Hope he grew in the form and quality of his composition, both prose and poetry. At the risk of appearing in the role of a "fond father," I venture the opinion that another ten years would have seen him writing for the world to read. We have found among his manuscripts lovely sonnets, plays for children, church-year productions, and a few stories, that will someday make his children very proud. I had hoped to arrange some of these for this book, as well as some of his letters to his mother and to me (before he met Corky's mother!). They are really classics in their field. He was a dreamer and a poet, he had a song, and there was in him "that rare fire"; but equally he was a friendly man of thoughtful, generous, constant action.

Of course, in some things he was not methodical—his brother Daniel declared that he never did get himself organized. Those two boys simply had to have separate rooms even when they were small, because in the same room there was a continuous battle and often a running fight over clothes—which is whose and where whose belongs. When I once told Clark that his pants looked better after hanging in the closet between midnight and dawn instead of jammed between the mattress and the foot of the bed, he replied, "Sure, but think of what a sweet disposition that would give Daniel; I've got to make a big, bold man out of him!" Of course, Corky's "Pretty Mummie Betty" finished the good work we had tried to begin, and Daniel presently had nothing on his brother Clark. When Betty came, a lovely well-groomed girl, into the life of our son, he had already made at least a beginning at organizing himself.

It was in a vacation time during those awkward, scrapping days when neckties were being misplaced and purloined that I was rudely torn from my shaving by the sound of violence in the living room. I found Daniel sitting on his brother's chest, though not too securely. Indeed an early change of position was in prospect when I tore the gladiators apart. To my command for an immediate explanation Daniel answered with a snort, "Aw, he's talking all the time about Peace and Brotherhood, and I'm sick of it. I told him it was soft stuff and he dove into my belly." It was a *Christmas* vacation and the boys were at home from prep-school. After a year at Oakwood, Clark thought himself philosophically a pacifist; but being still of a carnal nature, he was quite ready to fight for the faith that was in him.

Oakwood and the Quakers made a profound impression on Clark—an impression that registered deeply, permanently in his developing character. More than any other man I have known he qualified spiritually for membership in the "wider fellowship" of Friends. But after those first impressionable Oakwood days, he was never a pacifist. He was both a mystic and a realist, and as a realist who with great and growing eagerness followed Jesus and sought to know His will, he could not accept or support the absolute position, though always he respected and honored those of his intimates who did.

It was at this period of his life that our talks and "conferences" took on real proportions. As I so vividly remember them now, I am glad that I overcame all my natural propensities and, at times asserting "sublime" self-denial, was really a good listener. And it was not hard to listen to Corky's Daddy, because in addition to being from almost his first breath an incurable "arguer," he developed into a strong, fair debater and an entrancing conversationalist. How I miss him just across the desk, or in the Arizona Room and study, or walking down the Deering lanes! We shared with each other our convictions; and when he called for them, I gave him my reasons. He took them or left them, but eventually he arrived at his own, and always his were "with malice toward none and charity for all."

He accepted completely one family tradition; he never signed a pacifist pledge and always he opposed the circulation of such a statement among students and mentally immature young people. He believed that it was, however sincerely done, a "sin against youth." He accepted in his own right the family position; and it was to him, without prejudice to the opposite conviction of others whom he respected and loved, "both immoral and un-Christian to commit one's self to a specific act in advance of a particular event, the details of which cannot be known."

Always and constructively Clark was a man of peace and a peacemaker. Never could he in all the "world's wide border" hate any human being—any man, woman or child. In uniform one day I heard him deny the assumption that the American soldier must hate Germans to be a good soldier. Hate the evil system with all your might, yes; but not those who with us are equally, however misguided, its victims. The "love your enemies" of Jesus was real and timely to him. He did not dodge it. He loved his enemies, saying, "If our cause wins, they will be free, too. In this world you cannot isolate any evil or any good. We do not fight to win for ourselves and for our children any good that cannot be shared."

Idealistic? Yes, always Clark was that, but what he did about his ideals was always very real—rooming with the older man at Mt. Hermon, for instance; and finally, enlisting as a chaplain. Realistically he said, "Hate, a reasoned hate, corrodes the soul, makes a bad soldier. You cannot teach that to young Americans in one generation, nor in two. We won't hate people. It is love of America, love of freedom, love of home, love of justice, that will win for us. Lincoln proved that for Americans, proved and demonstrated it. Read what he said! "Certainly even at the beginning of his career as a chaplain, he distinguished between the swift and deadly passion of a supreme battle moment and this "reasoned hate." Yes, always he was a realist. For him there was about war itself nothing but ugliness. It was awful business thrust upon us—business that had to be done. But freedom, truth, human personality, were the holy things that had to be defended and preserved against war itself, and at whatever cost. For him there was no alternative and the only way out was the way ahead.

He was happy when Congress recognized the status of the conscientious objector. Then he was the more proud of America, but twice he said in effect, "The pacifist must not continue to be a pacifist now. He cannot talk and propagandize without helping the enemy, without in some measure at least hurting America and delaying the victory of freedom." If he could talk it over with me today, I am sure he would agree with the young lieutenant colonel whom I met in Assam in 1943. He had once been a student pacifist, but he said to me, "The preachers who persuaded student

o sign pledges as I was persuaded should go to the camps for
conscientious objectors, too—if they are among the few who have
not renounced the position as I had to."

I believe that had Clark been a pacifist, he would be in a camp
for conscientious objectors today. Yes, I am sure that, refusing the
exemption granted his high calling, he would have thus confirmed
his pacifist decision and either had his "witness" or gone to an
ambulance corps.

And now we are off to Rutgers. Clark came to his room in the
old Main Building of New Brunswick Theological Seminary, the
oldest institution of its kind in America, overlooking the Raritan
River, in the fall of 1931, and began two crowded years at "dear
old Rutgers." He did sound work in these two years at the university and made a few new friends, but for him the glow from
Hope was somewhat dimmed and I think that he was lonely. He
did outside literary work, for always he was a self-help student and
earned money to help carry his expenses. He formed one close
friendship at Rutgers with a Jewish boy, a blind student to whom
he read two or more hours every day and whom we came to know
and admire. Also he earned a man's wages on the farm—earned it
generally, but drew it *always*—and was never above hard work
of any kind.

At Oakwood he had been assistant baker and he held the same
position under our mother at Long House. I wish that you could
see him as often as I have seen him, sleeves rolled up to the elbows,
apron covering his front, and flour on his chin, kneading the great
loaves and shouting his favorite line: "Oh, Mother, always the
world is full of sin, sickness, and sorrow . . ." and then after a
pause he would finish with ". . . women!" But we never heard
the rest of it nor the last of that! And his singing voice was
something awful.

In Clark's last year at Rutgers he lived with my younger brother,
the Uncle Paul who had been a valet to his babyhood, a tutor in

his childhood—the Uncle Paul he deeply loved and greatly admired. Paul was now the minister of the First Presbyterian Church in Bound Brook, New Jersey, the husband of a lovely young wife Aunt Olive, and the father of two rugged lads, Charles and David —another pair not unlike Clark and his brother. Also there was a dog, a silver cocker spaniel named Tobey.

That dog, by the way, brought great confusion to Long House on a never-to-be-forgotten Sunday afternoon when the Polings were entertaining Governor Tobey of New Hampshire. Fearing some untoward incident our mother had locked the spaniel in the boys' dormitory. That subterfuge, that very lack of frankness brought on the disaster! Mary, missing the dog and not knowing about the arrangement, came shouting across the lawn right into the face of the distinguished visitor, "Here Tobey, here Tobey naughty boy, come and get your dinner!" Well, both Tobeys got their dinners that day, but perhaps one of them also got the shock of his public life.

Clark had a great year in Bound Brook with the Paul Polings. Always he was grateful for it and always Charles and David and their parents well remember their "boarder" who, in the words of his ministerial uncle, "made up in part for his recalcitrant youth by walking the dog and running the boys." I am sure that what he received from my brother and in my brother's house just about equalled all that he got in the distinguished university; and when in June, 1933, he graduated from the one, he left the other with a nostalgia of regret. Aunt Mabel and his Great Uncle Paul have a large place in Corky's life because of the large place they filled in the life of his father.

Yale 1936 is the Old Eli date of our son, for that is the year of his graduation from the Yale Divinity School. His three years in New Haven were certainly up until then the most fruitful years of his life. He saturated himself with the traditions, he captured the spirit, and now that I look back upon the period, I know that

he capitalized to great advantage on every opportunity. Pardon
me if I say it, but Corky's daddy was presently Yale Divinity
School at its best. Howard Conn was his closest friend at Yale and
became to the Seminary and to Clark's life work what Tubby had
been through Oakwood and college. Not that the first ever faded,
but Howard Conn was added and a challenging addition he became. Clark named Howard the finest student mind of his knowledge—brilliant, honest, hard-working, and adventurous. What
Howard Conn has written about Clark is so discerning and I believe so true, that I here pass it on to his children:

"Clark and I were so close all through Yale that I thought of
him as a brother. He had more life than any other member of his
class. It is perhaps fitting that he should be the first to move ahead
into the adventure of the life beyond. Yet his going is the keenest
personal loss to all who knew him and loved him. His place can
never be filled by anyone else. His sacrifice makes vivid the tragedy
of war, that the price war extracts is the best of human life.

"It was inevitable that Clark should have entered the chaplaincy.
He had such love for people that wherever people were in need,
he would be there in their midst to minister to that need. At
convocation this spring I talked with a boy whom I had first met
nine years ago when he was in grammar school and a member of
the little Methodist Church in South Meriden which Clark was
serving as student pastor during our first year in seminary. So
genuine was Clark's interest in the people of that little parish that
they knew he loved them, loved them and still loved them during
the years in which he moved on to serve two large and strong
churches. This grammar-school boy, moved by the inspiration of
Clark Poling, has now finished his first year as a divinity student,
giving himself likewise to the loving ministry of Jesus Christ.
Through him, as through many others of us who knew him, the
life of Clark will in some measure go on.

"He was a vibrant personality whose presence was felt in every

group. He possessed the best of the family traits, and had ca
pacities which some of us believed would give him even greate
usefulness. He had strength and magnetism, the warm love fo
people, the devoted passion for the Master. Yet beyond these
Clark had an intellectual swiftness and a breadth of appreciation
that took him into many fields—not in search of truth, for th
truth he had found in Christ; but in following and rejoicing in
the manifestations of this truth among scientists, poets, explorers
dramatists, and historians. Very few ministers read as widely and
as greatly as he did. And the great charm about Clark's study, a
about everything else that he did, was that it was without pla
and without system. It had the buoyancy, the spontaneity, and th
sparkle of the most intensely human personality I have ever known

"I have looked over the letters and papers which I have from
Clark out of our very close and deep friendship. There are severa
passages I should like to quote, but perhaps this from his Easte
1939 message to his church best expresses the freshness and th
depths of his faith:

'And spring is surely here! Put on your absurd and perky
bonnets. Throw off your winter coats and walk home from
your places of business. Look again at the world with fresh-
ened hearts and opened eyes. See beauty, forget ugliness. And
finally, beloved Christians, re-examine and remember rever-
ently your faith born of Christ; this is our Father's world and
no harm can befall, for we are His children. He does not fail,
and He is not mocked. In the joy of the resurrection.' "

And that was our son's message and that his eternal hope.

Yes, Clark was Yale at its best. In the first of this three year
he washed dishes at a downtown restaurant, walking four or fiv
miles a day to and from his work and meals. It was hard on hi
hands and shoes; it consumed valuable time; but he once said, "

gives me the common touch!" In the second or middle year, through the friendship of Dr. Hubert Jones who had been our family pastor at Port Washington on Long Island, and who was now District Superintendent of the Methodist Episcopal Church, Clark was given a student pastorate at South Meriden, Connecticut. Here his ministry really began. From the first he won the hearts of the people—all the people, as always he did. I stood only once by his side in that pulpit, but I shall never forget how love came up to him from the congregation. As I have written elsewhere, one of his Meriden boys whom he brought to Long House during a period of one summer vacation is now in Yale Divinity School.

All of Clark's last year at Yale was associated with the First Church of New London, Connecticut (Congregational), where he was student assistant to Rev. J. Romeyn Danforth, a man of rare intellectual and spiritual qualities. The relationship, both personal and organizational, was invaluable to the ministerial student. His mind began to flower; his leadership among children and young people was dynamic and fruitful; he wrote little plays, introduced pageantry, conducted a Bible class for young women at Connecticut College, and came to know that equally with preaching he would value and rejoice in the work of a pastor.

When Clark called in a home or office or whenever he sat with the sick, he was a shepherd of souls. Humble men and distinguished, the very young and the very old, and students especially found him and held him their understanding friend. All this really began in New London. I have met men in the Armed Forces at home and abroad who speak of his way with them, speak quietly and very slowly. One who had been a little child of his junior church in New London came weeping from her high-school class one morning after an announcement had been made by the teacher.

It was in this old First Church that Clark was ordained in the fall of 1936. That was a great night! There was the usual con-

ference with its questions and voting in the afternoon, and then
the public and formal service of ordination in the evening. Corky's
Great-Grandfather Poling of Portland, Oregon, was there for the
ordination prayer, and Dean Luther A. Weigle of Yale preached
the sermon. I gave the "charge" to the minister. My closing words
have now a significance that, of course, they could not have had
then:

"We have come into this historic church tonight to induct you
into your ministry, to charge you with your high calling. You face
an open door; you stand upon a threshold; but even so, and before
you enter that door and before I close this charge, I would call to
your attention three exits, three doors, the only three ways that
open out from your ministry.

"The first is the way of physical disability or of any honorable
retirement. The second is the way of repudiation. The third is the
way of triumph, the upward way, the way that is 'as the path of
the just that shineth more and more unto the perfect day.'

"As to retirement, I ask for you in the will of God the physical
heritage of your line. I ask for you a long and fruitful life. My
grandfather, your great-grandfather, was preaching in his eightieth
year. . . .

"As for repudiation, or any unworthiness, God grant that you
shall not be the first of your family to take that road. . . .

"But, my son, it is the third way, the way of triumph, the
shining path that holds my attention tonight as I think of you,
your ministry and its fulfillment. By this preaching, by this very
'foolishness' of preaching, the whole world is to be redeemed at
last. You are now to have a part in this redemption. May you so
preach and so minister, through long and fruitful years, that when
at last your earthly sun shall set, no cloud shall float upon your
sky."

A little later I shall tell of what Clark said at his ordination about
the virgin birth that was so fine and so characteristic. Well, when

hat night was over and our son was officially and formally what
or some time he had actually been, "Minister of the Gospel," a
"Pastor of the People," and a "Shepherd of the Flock," I was a
very happy man. Now my two sons, those "Poling kids," were
both with me in the high calling of our fathers. I could not reasonably have expected it and I had never even suggested it, but happy
was to find it so.

Clark's last days at Yale were just a little clouded—just a little
—but eventually the sun of his chosen profession shone even more
brightly because of the clouds. He graduated a member of his
class, but not with it. He alone of the seventy-seven did not receive
his diploma with the rest. The dean and faculty ruled that his
thesis was not properly completed, that it did not meet the requirements in time, but that he would receive his diploma in the fall,
provided the requirements were met, and so be graduated without
conditions a member of the class of 1936.

Clark never knew it, but I had a long talk with Dean Weigle.
Frankly, with all the evidence before me, I felt the ruling perhaps
unnecessarily severe, though not unfair. I would not have inter-
fered as a father, had that been possible, but never have I faced a
sterner father test. Clark was profoundly affected. He had not
believed it possible. Work in New London had multiplied; he had
also known an emotional experience of proportions that had en-
couraged delay, and at the end he had rushed things through (and
the faculty ruled) to a conclusion unworthy of him. His innate
fairness would not allow him to indict the decision, though he was
wracked and broken by it—the faculty never knew *how* wracked
and broken—and if ever my son had known how fully I knew
of his grief and how poignantly I shared it, he would have grieved
the more. But he was a good soldier, always he was that. He could
take it, and in the fall the diploma was his.

Presently the clouds began to lift; and before his son was born,
that particular sky was unbroken and I think serene. You see, "it's

not the fact that you're whipped that counts; but only how did you take it." Speaking of the incident, a Yale faculty member has said, "Perhaps one reason for Clark's having so early the most important pastorate of his class was this hard lesson learned without bitterness." That may be so.

Speaking of Clark's Yale days in a letter (appearing in the Postscript with other materials from the Divinity School files) Dr. Luther A. Weigle, Dean of Yale Divinity School, writes: " know of no one among these students of whose all-around fitness for the Christian ministry I have felt more sure than I was sure with respect to Clark. His initiative was tempered with a high sense of responsibility and his spontaneity with unusual regard for others. He had the impulsiveness of a great soul, yet he was dependable to the last bit of what the situation required."

Before I leave this particular portion of my story, there is Clark's journey to England in the summer of 1937, when he went as one of the youth representatives of Christian Endeavor to the Oxford Conference, and afterward cycled through England with Roy McCorkle, now associated with the Friends' Service Committee. I shall always regret not being with him in Oxford and even more, not having had time to receive the fuller report he was eager to give me, but the Conference broadened him, put a new note in his voice, and deepened his message. He was slow to appraise men and events unless quickly he felt justified in giving his support and endorsement. He was born with fairness in him but the wisest thing said about Oxford that I have heard—and one of the wisest things I have ever heard said about youth—Clark said when he returned from Europe in the fall of 1938: "Dad, there will never be a real world youth movement because we do not stay young long enough!"

He believed that youth would always infilter life; that they would be heard in church, in government, in human affairs everywhere; that they would be heard and felt as the young men

Alexander the Great and Alexander Hamilton and the Young Man of Galilee were heard and felt; but that they would decline segregation, or rather quickly outgrow it. As for Christian Endeavor and similar groups, he pointed out that they were invariably directed by adults—and he winked at me! He suggested that when real youngsters were out in front, they were put there by adults; and then he added with a grin, "You go ahead, Dad! You old boys lead the youth movement and we'll build the new world!"

Well, it is something like that; for wherever I go, I find youth directing affairs, organizing life, building the new world. They refuse to be confined to a "youth movement" and they do "age" and mature rapidly. All that I need to do is to remember that when my father was thirty-two he put on glasses. I recall that birthday because of that fact. I thought that he was a very old man—at thirty-two. Such matters are entirely relative and now my father at eighty-five is himself talking about "old men"—one of these, may I whisper in your ear, is just sixty-eight! Perhaps we are as old, not as our arteries, but as we think we are.

Even more significant than Oxford to Clark was England on a bicycle. Of that unforgettable summer experience Roy McCorkle has written me a letter. He tells of his voyage with Clark on the *DeGrasse* from New York; how they occupied the same cabin on their trip across the Atlantic and how at the Conference they decided to purchase bicycles and ride across the Midlands and into the Rhonda Valley, which is the coal mining section of Wales and perhaps the most under-privileged area of the British Isles. The boys had a few days together in London, with tea at the palace of the Archbishop of Canterbury. Then for a fortnight or longer they were in the open country. They covered as much as eighty to a hundred miles from dawn till dark, staying in youth hostels at night—they did not live expensively, and often they did their own cooking.

They stopped at the "Bruder Hof" of the Cotswolds—a

Christian community of Germans of utmost frugality and pessi
mism. Roy tells of one occasion when Clark became so intereste
in a group of attractive girls who were cycling toward them tha
he ran into the curb and tumbled into the grass, much to the
amusement of every one concerned. They spent one night in a
farmer's barn when they failed to reach the next hostel. In the
morning they had a delightful visit with the farmer and his family.
They separated at Plymouth—Roy sailing for America and Clark
going on into Devon to visit with the Morrows.

How eager Clark was to share with the family his summer
experience! Glad I am that even I caught a glimpse of the scene
he saw, and little snatches from the quiet adventures of tha
lingering quest.

He spent his last days in England with the Morrows, Honoré
Morrow and her daughters, in the fifteenth-century Devon farm-
house at Higher Brixham above the harbor where William of
Orange made his landing. It was with our dear friend Honoré that
he fought his battle over Spain—he wanted so much to go to Spain
with the Friends Service Committee. He wrote me with passionate
eagerness, but in the end wiser counsel prevailed and Honoré
Morrow was in that time his understanding friend. She was indeed
a wise and valiant woman, acquainted with grief and disappoint
ments, but never less than a conqueror. Her historical writings
and her Lincoln books especially, are among the most distinguished
in the American Library. Hers was a vision that swept the world
scene and saw life whole. She was a profound character. She was a
great woman. She became an early war casualty, for when her
heart was broken, what was left was not strong enough. Clark
found her while she was high in her great hope and came from her
with something fine and generous added to his youth.

He brought some presents from England. For his mother a
lovely shawl. For me an ancient small canvas—an old man stand

ng by the sea. He found the picture in a curio shop of a Devon own, where he and Honoré had gone, and he said as he handed to me, "Mrs. Morrow knew you would like it, Dad." An old man by the sea. . . . Yes, now I like it very much.

PLAY DAYS

OUR vacations were the high occasions of our family life. W
did everything but sell the family silver (really there wasn'
much!) to give Clark and his sisters and brother change of scen
and travel when they were growing up. We made deliberate choic
between saving a little to distribute among them in later life an
sharing with them, while they were children, study and experienc
at home and abroad. Of course, to move so large a family as our
so often, and frequently so far, was expensive; but our mother is
supermanager, and I put the extras from writing and speakin
into the travel treasury.

Nor let it ever be forgotten that friends have made life ver
wonderful for us—true friends who with unfailing love an
thoughtfulness have lifted us across the hard places. When sicknes
came and sorrow, or an unforeseen emergency, friends have don
for us what we could not do for ourselves. From them we hav
learned and received what we have sought to pass on to others; no
could we have completed such work as we have done had they no
been with us. And it was young Clark's friendliness that made h
life radiant, that won him in all age-levels such a host of friend
and that made of his life so great a blessing to so many. After livin
a good many years, I am sure that each of us has just as man
friends and as true as he deserves—and some of us have man
more than we could have deserved.

Some of those first summers were spent on the old Ohio far
where Clark's first mother was born, and there was a trip clear

the Pacific Coast across the United States and back through Canada, and many other shorter journeys—all before he could clearly remember. Both he and his brother and later their first baby sister were early on the road.

Our first extended vacations were in the Christian Endeavor Summer Community on Cape Cod, where the children came to know the great men and women of Christian Endeavor: Francis E. Clark, the founder, the "Good St. Francis" of the world's youth; and Mrs. Clark, just as good and as great; William Shaw, the "Field Marshal" of the society; Amos R. Wells, the editor; and scores of their contemporaries. On the sands of Sagamore "the Poling kids" began their more vigorous exploits. Also they made discoveries, among them a clam bed—fine white clams, if you please—that had not been found there before. Two of the adventures, however, might have had a tragic ending.

One day the very small brothers went on a long walk up the beach with their sister, who had just begun to toddle. The tide was coming in. Well, when I set out to overtake them, Daniel saw me coming and he put on all his steam to keep out of my reach. We were all but trapped by the in-rushing water. The only explanation that ever I got for that ordeal was "We wanted to see things!" Clark was not talking much then or there would have been much more said, for he was always the great explainer.

The second, and even more serious experience, came in a later summer when I was away from home, during the reign of Aunt Mabel. Fortunately, while I was absent, my younger brother Paul, Clark's uncle, was spending his summer with our family. Daniel was now nearly ten years old. With a lad of his own size and age, he had assembled some driftwood and made a flimsy raft. Anchored to the beach it made an ideal play boat, but a risky foundation it was for any voyage. Of course, the raft was a secret. It was not discovered until, swept out by the treacherous tide of Cape Cod Bay, it was a mile off shore and breaking up. My brother pulled a strong oar and got to the raft, or what was left of it, in time—just in time. He found Clark's brother in the middle of the driftwood, holding his friend tightly, realizing instinctively, I suppose, that they must not become panicky and slide into the water.

It was that experience that taught me the infinite value of the "ones!" I came home, having missed all telegrams, without knowing of our near family tragedy. A new man was driving the bus that ran from the station to the beach, and I became just a little impatient with his loquaciousness, for I was eager to finish the journey. Then suddenly I realized that he was talking about children, Sagamore summer children and a near tragedy that had come to two of them. I know now that the tale picked up a good deal in his telling, but what a difference—what a tremendous difference it made to me when he said, "One of the boys was Poling's kid." Then I wanted to hear everything and the rest of the journey was a torture of delay.

Ever since that evening one, *one human being,* has meant much more to me than any "one" ever meant before. Years afterward I read an editorial in a London journal describing a sinking in the North Atlantic with the loss of a ship from a convoy, and the article concluded, "And so after all, the loss was infinitesimal." The writer was thinking of war's grand strategy, the total of all losses, and the "Ultimates of Freedom"; but I thought of individual lives and homes, and I remembered the raft on the bay of Cape Cod, and I said to myself, "Infinitesimals? No, not infinitesimals, but Infinite Ones." And in that is the genius of freedom and democracy and the uniqueness of the Gospel of Christ which was to become the purpose and passion of Clark's life.

Our last vacation on Cape Cod was in the summer of 1919, the summer that brought us Clark's "second mother." In 1920 we were at home on Long Island, and small boys began to do odd jobs about the house and yard and to work in vegetable gardens

Also we swam in the Bay and fished off the shore. In 1921 we went for the first time to Lake Sunapee in New Hampshire, and that was also the summer of "the accident."

The accident was nearly the end of our summers together. Driving down from the Lake on the morning of July 4, after stopping for early breakfast in Greenfield, Massachusetts, we ran head-on into a telephone pole on the highway eight miles out of Northampton. Children playing by the road, a honey bee, and a faulty steering gear conspired to produce the disaster. Our mother, Rachel, Daniel, and Corky's daddy were all thrown clear of the car.

There were broken bones and other serious injuries followed by weeks in the hospital, but in the end a complete recovery for all—and that was little short of miraculous. A brave story it is, with Mother the heroine. Eventually we finished that vacation in New Hampshire as we began it, and our very suffering brought us all closer together. My brother Paul was with us, and our faithful nurse Nell Hostettler. My father and mother came on for a visit from Pennsylvania, and our "mother's helper," whom Billie named "Ge Ge," resigned as dietitian at the hospital to live in our home.

Clark's most serious injury was a broken leg just below the hip, and for a time that leg was shortened; but being a small boy with sound health, he completely outgrew the injury. He was a good patient, too, and did not whimper when the leg was set and re-set and he was kept sweating between sand bags through hot July and August days. Always he had a sense of humor, too, and the wink that never failed to produce results. His Uncle Albert had come hurrying from New York; after he had visited the scene of the wreck, he said to Clark, "If your dad had swerved that car eighteen inches, you would have landed in a tobacco field as flat as a floor."

"Yes, Uncle," was Clark's reply, "but you know Dad—how he does hate tobacco!" And then he winked!

That summer was followed by a winter in New York, and then in the spring of 1922, my vertebra having been fractured in the accident, I took a year's leave of absence from my New York church and we all went out to the desert—to Holbrook, Arizona —and to one of the most wonderful experiences that ever a family had. Almost a year was spent in the sun and romance of America's great Southwest. Again we were fortunate in our friends—many of them new friends we found among the pioneers and traders of Navaho land. We spent much of the time in the open, driving our ramshackle cars to all points of the compass and turning back the pages of history to live in the storied past. We hunted and we dug in the ruins of ancient pueblos. As strength returned, we climbed mountains and followed old trails.

Uncle Paul was still with us, and he tutored the boys until they entered the local school. (Clark's brother has his grade-school certificate from Holbrook.) Uncle Paul also began his preaching in the village church, with six small children and their yet smaller sister as a very considerable proportion of his total congregation. Two boys were hot partisans of the youthful parson and even suggested that he was almost as good as his elder brother, their father. However, their endorsement varied from time to time as the younger preacher stirred their ire with his class-room discipline.

Three Indian ponies came into the family in those Holbrook days—and many rabbits. The ponies were as sturdy and also as treacherous as Indian ponies frequently are, and the rabbits suffered from too much handling. Daniel had one memorable day when his hens produced an average of two eggs per fowl! But a "foul" trick it was—a foul trick of Clark's, who swiftly carried the eggs back to the nests as fast as his brother carried them in. And he was aided and abetted by Uncle Paul.

Yes, wonderful were our Arizona days together—days on the desert, days among the cedars and piñons and in the pine forests of the White Mountains. We cooked our meals in the Dutch oven over the open fire. We gathered nuts in their season and found beautiful rugs and pottery specimens in trading posts and "hogans." We told our Abram and David stories, and I wrote my first novel. Also we dreamed a dream of riches, riches from oil wells that always were just about to "come in!" Once we were lost in the desert after an unsuccessful grizzly bear hunt that took us far into the "Four Corner" country. The Navaho has his own ideas about signs, and sometimes to mislead the evil spirits that he believes are riding hard after him, he will turn signs around, make them point off in wrong directions, or lay them flat on the ground. Well, on that trip we ran into the work of a superstitious Indian and when finally, driving by the moon and stars, we reached Indian Springs, we had traveled trails never before known even to a Ford. Miserable was the experience, but one now pleasant to remember because of the family ties it strengthened.

We had gone to the desert to find strength for New York, strength to return, and so in the spring of 1923 we were again in the East and that summer and the summers of 1924-25 were spent in the cottage on beautiful Lake Sunapee that we had come to love. Corky would have been delighted with the perilous swing that, anchored to the great beech tree, carried us high above the down slope of the hill out toward the water; the wide veranda where the children played in stormy weather; the canoeing; and the surf-board-riding behind the small motor boat we rented. There were water sports and hikes into the country round about, fishing expeditions and long climbs to the top of the mountain from which the lake takes its name. There were picnics and wiener roasts on the island and countless tramps and rides to the village. Once as demure Ann sat cuddled against me and as we came down the steep hill into the town, she said, "Daddy, now we are in the underskirts of the village." Always she was great on new words. And Ann, among the sisters, was the pal of her younger brother. Theirs was a beautiful comradeship.

At one summer regatta the Buckhaven "four" took first place in the canoe race. There was something of a furor over that event, when it was discovered that the fourth "man" in the boat was a girl—blonde little Mary! Clark and his brother and their male friend had found in the small sister a better paddler than their own sex could at the moment produce; and so, with hair tucked under a cap pulled down to her nose, she stroked the crew to victory.

Mary was likely to do things like that. She was a better horse-back rider than her brothers; and in the University of Vermont a few years later she became captain of the women's rifle team, a team that won the National Intercollegiate Championship and whose captain won the War Department's 98.7 per cent marks-manship medal.

Mary has jotted down some impressions of the lad who sat in front of her in the canoe on that memorable regatta day:

Earliest recollections at Sagamore—Playing house with the toads and fearful of catching warts from them. Squashing blackberries in our mouths and all over our faces and boasting how we could walk barefoot over the rough ground.

Adventurous spirit—A canoe rigged up as a sailboat with Clark squatted low, racing back and forth across the bay with no concern for the oncoming storm.

We shared a trophy—Clark dared to include me in his crew for an Indian war canoe race—one girl among all boys. We won the race!

Generosity—Clark invested in many books which he loved. I saw him reading an especially nice edition of *The Canterbury Tales* with Rockwell Kent illustrations. I admired it. On Christmas, several days later, I received the book from Clark as a gift. On the inside cover were his name with the date and "To Mary from Clark." I knew he had given me one of his very own.

Always ready for a good time—One vacation I was met by Clark with "Want to see the best movie you ever saw?" I said,

"Sure, but how do you know it's good?" "I've already seen it once." So we went to the memorable *It Happened One Night* and had a wonderful time.

Letter received before being married—Since we were married while Dad and Mother were rounding the world, my older brother Dan married us. Clark felt a certain responsibility for this step I was taking. He wrote me a letter wishing me all happiness and promising his help if I were ever in need of it! I have always been grateful.

Christmas 1941—Upon seeing our "Phil" at one year, he could not contain himself, but burst out laughing because Phil was so round and fat—not unlike Clark himself at that age. His comment I remember was "You're a good mother."

Letter received after Nancy was born—Congratulations from Clark while he was at Camp Shelby and a rebuke that she was named Nancy and not Mary, which is a very beautiful name."

Clark clerked for part of one season in Morgan's General Store and Post Office at the Buckhaven landing, and among the many happenings that made the experience worth while was his memorable bout with tobacco. We had talked the tobacco business over rather fully in the family and, remembering my own boyhood, I had never promised the boys that proverbial thrashing if ever I caught them smoking. But they did know how I felt about it and why. Also they agreed with me that since eventually they had the decision to make and since I affirmed that if they decided to smoke, I would neither manhandle nor disown them, however badly I might feel, we would talk things over "man to man" before they "cast the die."

Well, one day after lunch Clark came to me, half-ashamed, half-defiant, but direct: "Dad," he said, "I'd like to smoke—not cigarettes, but cigars, and later a pipe. I'd like to try it out now—just try it out, you know." (He was fourteen.)

"All right," I replied, "why not try it out—you're set on cigars, are you?"

He nodded, "Yes, I prefer cigars, but Mr. Morgan won't let me have them unless you say O.K.; you'll have to buy them, Dad!"

And I did that afternoon. At the supper table Clark manifestly was uneasy. He had decided to take the canoe after supper and go out on the lake for his first tryst with Lady Nicotine. Yes, I was shameless; I allowed him to go *after* supper. At the time he was sleeping in the garden house behind the cottage, and perhaps an hour after he embarked upon his more or less secret adventure, I heard him come in. He was not hard to hear! It is possible that boys have been sicker after their first smoke—yes, possible—but my second-born was SICK! In his own language—his own broken and interrupted testimony when I went out to him—he was "Poisoned! Dying! Get the doctor! Yes, sir. Get all the doctors unless you want to call the undertaker first." I did my best to atone for what I had done, and eventually matters quieted down.

In my own case a good many years before, that first experience had been intensified by half-ripe tomatoes eaten as I came staggering up from the barn through Mother's garden—green tomatoes swallowed in the wild hope that they would keep other things in place. Well, they didn't, they just didn't. Mother came to the conclusion that her first-born was having a hemorrhage. . . .

When Clark came out of the garden house the next morning, he found me in the bathroom shaving. "Dad," he queried, "did it do that to you?"

I nodded my head and rubbed in the lather.

There was silence for a second; then he turned on his heel and shot a typical last word over his shoulder, "What a nut your son's father was!"

And that was the end of that, though his final decision regarding tobacco stood upon firmer foundations than a rocking stomach.

We had grand neighbors at Sunapee and of these the nearest

were the Crosses—Dean Wilbur Cross of the Yale Graduate School, Editor of the *Yale Quarterly Review,* and after his "retirement" three times Governor of Connecticut. Our boathouses adjoined and we had many family affairs together. In the spring of 1924 a mother skunk set up a maternity ward under the Cross front porch, which for the "duration" became sacred to her and her family of seven. It was a sight as well as a smell to see Mother Skunk take off in the morning with her family, leading them in single file down the path to the water's edge. After drinking and washing, playing the while, they would come sedately back to their home under the porch. They were never molested. And not once did they take advantage—any other advantage—of Dean Cross's hospitality; indeed their deportment was better than that of the young humans just over the fence. But at any rate Clark and his brother had "enjoyed" one skunk experience and they had no stomach for another. Then one morning the family was gone. There was for a time just the suggestion of a thank-you note left behind, but they were never offensive and we missed them.

Clark had one bout with a bee at Sunapee that proved him allergic to stings; in a few minutes his eyes swelled shut and he puffed up like a man with dropsy. Again it was Mother who found the antedote and saved the patient. Always he was dodging bees and poison ivy. Frequently he was called a "whited sepulcher" because he was plastered with lead ointment, but no allergy ever kept him from following a trail or exploring a wilderness.

Our family never got over Sunapee. Not even the farm, Long House with its added attractions and more enduring qualities, could blot out memories of that most beautiful of all New Hampshire lakes. We always looked forward to picnic days when we returned.

In 1925, following the International Christian Endeavor Convention in Portland, Oregon, and a visit with Clark's Oregon grandfather, we went to Alaska. On July 13, a Friday, we sailed from Vancouver, B. C. That was a voyage, for not a cloud shut out the sun and scarcely a ripple disturbed the "Inside Passage." We were told that ours was the first good trip of the season, and better than good it was, for we had uninterrupted pleasant weather and perfect views of some of the world's finest scenery.

At Ketchakan we left the steamer and were met by Rev. Marsden, Indian minister of the Presbyterian Church in the Indian town of Metlakatla on the Island of Annetta. This is the famous community founded by "Father" Duncan and bought by him from British Columbia nearly a century ago. We were carried by the Marsden tug sixteen miles off the mainland to the Marsden home, where in a comfortable apartment on the second floor of the large house we spent one of the memorable vacations of our life together. Rev. Marsden was a graduate of Marietta College in Ohio and of Lane Theological Seminary in Cincinnati. With Mrs. Marsden, a very gracious lady, to assist him, he made the ideal host. Their beautiful daughter Marietta and her husband Edward Benson are among our never-forgotten friends.

Now the "Poling kids" were really "at home." They reverted to type. Swimming, fishing, or hunting with the perfectionists in all of these sports was the order of every day. And at the risk of having these lines censored, I am telling you that all of us, including our mother, got F-A-T. For the first and only time her weight equaled that of her husband. Salmon livers, Indian meal, trout and venison, with now and then a baked seal, were our regular menu. The longest hikes and heaviest work could not counteract that diet! Of course, travel between the Island and mainland and between islands was by motorboat. With the boys, directed by the Marsdens and their friends, I was constantly traveling. We visited deserted villages where weathered totem poles were silent sentinels of the past. We went on a wild but unfruitful brown bear hunt, and once Clark and I waited on a great rock off shore while seal and otter, led by an irresistible curiosity, swam close or snorted about us.

Once when a tourist steamer from California docked briefly at Metlakatla to give its passengers a glimpse of the native village, the director of the party pointed to the gaping "Poling kids" and said, "There you have the 'breeds,' the mixed bloods of the Island." And did those breeds love it! That will always be a family tradition. And "breeds" we are—Dutch, German, Irish, Welsh, Scottish, and English. My father declares that he gets his conservatism from the Scots, his stubbornness from the English, his suggestion of melody from the Welsh, and his extreme modesty from the Irish."

The great event of that Alaska summer was the marriage of Uncle Paul. Olive, his "Dearest," the girl he met at Willamette University in Oregon, had gone with us to Metlakatla, and late in the summer he followed her there. One September evening they were married in the Indian church. I was assisted by Rev. Marsden. Rachel was maid of honor and Daniel was best man. The rest of the family with Marietta and other Indian young people played their various parts. There were cut flowers from Ketchakan, but lovelier flowers from the tundra. The village band led the wedding procession to the church and back again, and then played for the reception. In the Marsden home, directed by the head of the house, we spent a never-to-be-forgotten evening with ancient men of the Tribe, talking in their own tongue of yet more ancient tribal customs. At the last the bride and groom were inducted with solemn ritual into tribal membership and given Tsimpshean names. Now always on the Island of Annetta they have a refuge; and if ever they are homeless or in want, Metlakatla is their haven; for never can anyone be hungry or roofless there, unless all are roofless and hungry.

We left the Marsdens and our summer idyl to journey by motorboat, steamer, and transcontinental limited four thousand miles down the sea and across a continent. The village dock was filled with our Tsimpshean friends, and the high hill was green above them as we chugged away. Faces faded first, and at last the lovely Island sank below the horizon; but evermore we shall see the village and its gracious people, evermore remember Metlakatla.

We returned by way of the Canadian Rockies, visiting Jasper National Park and also our mother's brother in Winnipeg. Clark especially rose to these occasions, for always he found satisfaction in new scenes and new friends, though never was any boy more loyal to old scenes and old friends.

In 1926 we were on the good ship *Carmania* en route to London and the World's Christian Endeavor Convention, which was held in the famous Crystal Palace, the largest building (or rather buildings) of glass ever erected. The palace burned years ago. We had rented the old rectory in Shoeburyness, Essex, at the mouth of the Thames—on the great estuary. The ancient house stood by the church, which in turn stood upon foundations of a Roman temple. We came directly by taxi from the boat train and London. With our trunk on top and our excited peering children inside, we roused the countryside. Parking the children in the rectory, our mother and I attended the convention. Clark and Daniel also got some of the convention—perhaps more than they wanted! A remarkable convention it proved to be, with German delegates present—the first German delegation to attend an international gathering of any kind following World War I.

After the convention the American delegation visited the continent of Europe. In Holland, Germany, Austria, Switzerland, Italy, and France, Clark, his brother, his sister Rachel, and Virginia Tuxill who was as another sister, saw for the first time sights and scenes of which they had read and perhaps dreamed. Corky will have pictures of that expedition which concluded with a trip by air from Paris to London—the family's first adventure of that kind. It might have been the last, for another ship, caught in the storm that delayed us for thirty minutes, crashed in a hayfield just behind Dover.

For the rest of the summer I occupied the pulpit of Christ Church in Westminsterbridge Rd., London, having exchanged pulpits with my friend Dr. William C. Poole, who was preaching for me in the Marble Collegiate Church in New York. During the week between Sundays, we explored the metropolis of the world, or played tennis on the deep rectory lawn, or visited the castle ruins, or tramped the beaches, or hiked the trails of Sussex and Essex and Hampshire with new found friends—friends who remain to this day. Clark, though he was younger, entered eagerly the conversations with the Cambridge boys who had their own ideas about how "America won the war" and the payment of war debts. At any rate, it was agreed in those days that the war had been won, and that the peace would last. How well we knew—or thought we did—so little!

The family particularly rejoiced in an institution new to them— English "tea"—and whenever it came that "time," we ate and drank everything in sight to the amazement and perhaps disgust of the English servants whom we had "leased" with the house. Clark's capacities for both thought and food were from the beginning Continental; he and his juvenile contemporaries were ever ready for the next meal—their stomachs were never full. I developed a definite inferiority complex and could never look the cook in the eye.

Clark's sisters, Jane and Billie, were at the age of quick entrances and exits. They were everywhere and anywhere. On shipboard our mother put each of them into a harness and kept them on the leash, but at Shoeburyness they had the run of the lawns and gardens and they ran themselves and "Ge Ge" thin.

Our last English days were spent in the famous spa, Cheltenham, where we went to visit the Bromages and where we found lovely Joan. That gave us another July birthday—the ninth;

Billie's comes on the twenty-ninth and Jane's on the twenty-seventh. We journeyed directly to Southampton from Cheltenham and sailed for home on the *Coronia*. It was a stormy crossing, greatly enjoyed by Clark and Daniel, but a terrible ordeal for our new sister. To Joan, even as she remembers it now, it was a sort of living death. I carried her out and I carried her in, but she declares that wherever she was, she always was inside out!

Joan writes of her brother Clark: "Coming from England, I was a bit bewildered by seven new brothers and sisters. However, each one was a distinct personality and for me, Clark stood out among them all. He was always so gay! Everyone was happy when Clark was there. How he teased the aunts and all of us! Once at Christmas Aunt Tillie was asleep in her chair right under the tree. I had received a gift of bright red fingernail polish and while Aunt Tillie dozed, Clark covered each of her nails with my polish. Imagine her surprise when she awoke. It was her first and last experience with polish! When I grew up, my boy friends came to the house on Broad Street in Philadelphia and I can see Clark as he would hurry down the stairs just to greet Reid, now my husband, as "Jack" or "Ted," knowing all the time exactly who Reid was. It made me furious, of course, for I didn't want "the one man" to think that any others counted. Clark got his biggest kick when I was embarrassed by two friends arriving at the same time. He deliberately changed their names! Corky had a wonderful dad; it became my ambition to find a husband who measured up to him."

After England and Europe came Long House. We had purchased the old pre-Revolutionary farm sometime before that eventful overseas journey; and while we were away, it was being prepared for the coming of its new family. Never again would any of us greatly care to roam, though roam we did. Very quickly we became jealous of any interruptions of our New Hampshire vacation days. Perhaps when Clark's sisters were small, blueberry picking almost wearied them of the hilltop and its "Blueberry Mountain," for ours is just about the blueberry kingdom of New England, but even those ordeals were forgotten when the fire swept high in the Arizona Room and song and laughter filled Long House.

As school days became more crowded and college came and then divinity school, Clark had less time for free vacations—there was work to do. But he never lost the urge to come to his family and to be where they were. One vacation trip of this later period Daniel and I will never forget. We drove down to the Cape and, after a visit with Mother Clark on the farm at Sagamore, came on to Martha's Vineyard, parked our car, and took the steamer to Nantucket—that most romantic bit of all New England. Two nights we spent together in the ancient whaling town or on its beaches, visiting the museums, studying the houses, walking the cobbled streets, bathing in the surf, and resting on the sand.

On the second night, under the stars that seemed so very low I lay stretched between my sons and listened—listened as I had not listened since they were little boys. Now each was a man in his own right, a man with his work in the world. I did not know that never again would we be as we were then and that only once again would we three tramp together. But I listened as though it were a last time. They razzed each other, threw pebbles at each other across their father—and too many of their shots fell short! But do not give me your sympathy, for I could still take care of myself. Their conversation ran the gamut of church and school and state. They debated the universe and talked about their girl friends, and still I listened. (Believe it or not, and our mother hardly will!)

I listened, listened and dozed, until the day turned its midnight and the silver moon arose, and still they talked. Theology it was that finally got me started! Not that I am a theologian, but after Clark had challenged Daniel with a particularly radical assumption and after his elder brother had denounced him as a son of heresy and a "Yale liberal," I ventured the prophecy that I would live to see the day when the "Princeton conservative" would find himself to be no less evangelical than his argumentative younger brother. That suited neither of them, and so they rolled me in the sand— or tried to. And then arm in arm we strolled up the beach. Deliciously weary and sleepy, we at last went to bed. Some day I shall take my grandchildren down to Nantucket and stretch on that beach and talk.

"DADDY, I'M GOING TO PREACH"

I HAVE just had a good visit with Corky, and as I write today the snow is white and shining on the Catskills across the Hudson. Corky's father greatly loved this beautiful river with the mountains rising beyond.

On his own initiative Corky slept with me last night. I had put him to bed and told him a story earlier in the evening before going out to a meeting. He was not happy about that departure, not at all happy, but stood in the upstairs window waving. He does not like "going away" unless he is going, too. And in that he is a normal small boy, but with something added—because he has waited so long for one to return. When we came back, he was soon awake; and when I was ready to retire, he was ready to change beds. He sat up with sleep-filled eyes and watched me get into my pajamas; and when the light was out, he came very close, put his small right arm cross my chest, and said, "Hold my hand, Granddaddy, and tell me Black Sambo story." And though the hour was very "early," he had his story and fell quietly asleep. But when I disengaged his hand, he remonstrated; and so I fell into my first doze holding his hand. I dreamed that he was his daddy—and, of course, he is.

Today I am writing about Clark's choice of a task and of his high calling. When he was a small boy, he said, "I'm going to be a lawyer," and I rather liked the idea. His brother Daniel ran true to the family tradition from the beginning. Always he was looking ahead to the day when he would preach, and no escapade ever dimmed for him that vision, though I am bound to admit that some of them seriously disturbed mine. At college he refrained from joining the "Ministerium," made up of pre-theological candidates because, as he explained in answer to my question, "I don't want to embarrass the Brethren." That some of the rest of us were at times greatly embarrassed by his attitude may have troubled him, but not too much.

Clark was determined to break, as he frequently expressed it, "the vicious circle of father to son, and when the son becomes a father, then father to son again." He seemed to have every natural instinct of the lawyer and a few more, and perhaps because even I had begun to feel the monotony of the father-to-son business, I gave him real encouragement. An experience that may have had a bearing on what happened later was the vacation he spent at Mt. Lawn, *Christian Herald's* beautiful summer home for under-privileged children at Nyack, overlooking the Hudson. With his sister Ann, he went to Mt. Lawn and served through the season as a senior counsellor. His love for children and his maturing purpose to make his life count somewhere for human gains and for a fuller life for others, were definitely enriched and broadened at Mt. Lawn.

As I remember Clark's boyhood now and even his prep-school days, I realize that in spite of all he said and even believed at the time, he was always preparing for the ministry. His major questions were generally in the realm of Christian faith and practice; and when he was most argumentative, he was hammering someone —frequently his mother or father—with theological matters.

Two experiences of this period are especially significant now. The first came in his third year at Oakwood, and the second just before he graduated there. One Friday afternoon I received a telegram that read: "Meet me Grand Central eleven tomorrow. Very important. Don't tell Mother. I'm not going home. Love. Clark." That was his first telegram, and to say the least it left me uneasy.

Peremptory it was to be sure, but the "Don't tell Mother" and "I'm not going home" were the disturbing clauses. What kind of a jam was he in? Well, I thought of many things; and the more I thought, the more troubled I became. You may be sure that I was waiting at the train gate when eleven o'clock in the morning came.

Clark was, I think, the first passenger through. He did not have the usual infectious smile that was always good to see. (His smile and a quick nervous laugh, equally infectious, were characteristic of him; those who heard that laugh seemed always to remember it.) He flung his hands out and kissed me. Poling men and also men of Corky's mother's family are reared in that ancient form of salutation. With both our families it is Germanic rather than French—not a side-swiping double-cheek affair, but an unsanitary smacker full in the mouth.

"Let's go to the office," he said, "You didn't tell Mother?"

With a guilty feeling I nodded a "Yes" on the question, and we went directly to the study in the Marble Collegiate Church.

The study, then as now, is long and narrow in its dimensions and secluded in its location. My flat-top desk was in the far end at the windows which look out on Fifth Avenue. Clark turned back to shove a chair under the doorknob, since there was no key. I was impressed by the gesture, but not reassured. I sat down. He came and at once dropped into a chair directly opposite. Lowering his chin into his cupped hands, he searched my face. I remember that moment even now as one of the longest and most uncertain moments of my life. I thought of many things; what could it be that shut out his mother and home? I was not a happy father as I watched Clark's very dark eyes, but one mistake I did not make— I did not ask any questions; I did not begin the conversation; I did what is hardest—I waited.

And then the boy across the table came to life; he looked even more intently into my eyes and said, "Dad, what do you know about God?" Just that and nothing more. Well, after what I had expected, knowing not what to expect, that was a relief, but an even greater surprise.

Let me write here that to Clark I was first "Daddy" and then interchangeably and for no particular reason that I ever isolated "Daddy" or "Dad." The last time I saw him and the last time he called to me it was "Daddy!" There were other times, generally moments of mock solemnity with implications of my accumulating years and decreasing speed, when he would call me with a broad accent, "F-a-t-h-e-r." But that was almost ecclesiastical in connotation. Now in the quiet study, to the boy with his old but to him immediate and personal question, I was "Daddy."

What *did* I know about God? I am glad that the question took me by surprise, without warning; that I had no chance to prepare an answer, to get ready for him. For that question of a boy in one of his first major emotional as well as intellectual experiences, only an intuition—and perhaps a father's intuition—had the answer. I know now that my answer was for us both the one and only answer that could have satisfied the questioner. Whatever else it lacked, it was completely honest.

"Clark," I replied, repeating the question, "what do I *know about* God? Mighty little." That startled him. He straightened, but held my eyes as I went on: "Mighty little do I know about God—less now than I thought I knew when I sat where you sit! But, Clark, what I do know by the test of experience—sickness and health, disappointment and success, sorrow and joy, death and life—what I do *know* about God changes my life."

There we began and there after several hours we left the great matter. Yes, and there we often returned through the following years.

We had our lunch together in the city and then went home to our mother. Exactly why he didn't want his mother to know, I never knew; but I imagine he had feared another conclusion of the interview that would have made her unhappy. He was very thoughtful and he would not hurt anything or anyone unless it just had to be done. Corky has had some escapes from discipline because at a very early age he discovered and exploited that quality! But our homecoming was one of the happiest of a long series. His mother said that even as we came into the house she knew something fine had happened, that something new had come to us both, bringing us closer together; and she always afterward affirmed that our father-son relations were more vital and intimate from that Saturday afternoon. Years afterward Clark answered that same question for someone in Schenectady, and Betty and I found the answer among his miscellaneous papers. I shall write about that later, but in his own fine phrases it is the same answer.*

The second of these experiences was timed in much the same way, and again we sat together in the long study. But this time there was no command not to tell mother. Again the boy sat with his cloven chin cupped in his hands, looking across the desk at the man. Now it was not a question but a challenging affirmation: "Dad," he said, "I don't believe the virgin birth!"

That ran true to form. He more frequently than not challenged for an answer with an affirmation, but sometimes the affirmation was seriously meant, and this was one of the times. Again I was glad to be taken by surprise. Again I had no "prepared manuscript." Again I spoke out of my knowledge of him, rather than from the wisdom of books or the creeds of the Fathers. Again I was first his father, who had his own unanswered questions, and I said, "Well, then that settles it. If you don't, you just don't. You cannot make yourself believe—even if you greatly desire to believe —any more than you can make yourself happy or make yourself fall in love. But, Clark, are you sure you are ready to say that? Intellectually sure?"

* "An Answer to a Question"—Postscript, page 142.

His brow contracted and, waiting an instant, he came back with the question: "What do you mean by that?"

"I mean," I answered him, "that unless you have read the books, unless you have searched the pages and listened to the masters who have thought in this field—I mean that unless both intellectually and spiritually you are justified in your conclusion, that affirmation will bring you unnecessary confusion and embarrassment. Yes, are you ready to say it?"

He lifted his eyebrows, grinned, and said, "Daddy, where are the books?"

Aside from any books he may have had, I gave him two—one from the pen of Robert E. Speer, *The Deity of Jesus,* and another, perhaps the most convincing, direct argument for the virgin birth, written by Charles E. Jefferson. Not until his ordination day did I know what impression the books made, for we never discussed the subject again—not even when he returned the books. On that occasion he just slapped me on the shoulder and grinned. But when among his ordination questions he was asked: "Do you believe the virgin birth?" he had an answer that was direct and courageous. It was hard for him to give his answer in the old parish church of New London with his fundamentalist grandfather, whom he loved and greatly admired, right in front of him; hard for him to speak with his mother and father listening in.

Clark may have had some poor answers, but he was not one to dodge hard questions, and he said, "My ministry stands on Jesus Christ. To me God is limitless, and for Him the virgin birth would be as simple as any natural birth. But it is not unique, for nearly every Eastern religion claims as much for its founder—Buddhism, for instance. Surely faith in the virgin birth is not the ultimate, or all the Gospel writers would have made the claim. Paul would have affirmed it, and Jesus Himself would not have remained silent. He did not leave his unique relationship to God the Father undeclared; 'the Father and I are one,' he said.

Deity and the virgin birth are not synonymous. The vicarious atonement does not stand upon it. I do not disbelieve, but I am not convinced." And then with a glance in my direction, he quoted one of his father's favorite verses from St. Paul: "For He hath made us able ministers of the New Testament, not of the letter but of the spirit, for the letter killeth but the spirit giveth life."

There was just the suggestion of appeal in Clark's glance and he got from me what he looked for! Even his grandfather was satisfied—and who would not have been? Clark had read my books well, but he had done vastly more than read many books; he had "searched the scriptures" and pledged his mind to intellectual honesty. His ministry never said to any man, "Take it or leave it according to my interpretation or belief." Always his invitation was the invitation of Jesus: "Come and see." And he never failed to practice what he quoted that day in New London at his ordination—"The letter killeth but the spirit giveth life."

He was vividly an evangelical with a searching mind unafraid of truth! From having been theologically a liberal, he moved in a few years toward the middle position; and as I have suggested elsewhere, he and his conservative brother Daniel stood together rather than apart when last we three talked things over. But one thing never changed: always he was God's man and his own, and neither from his father nor any other did he take his convictions and conclusions. His radiant Christian experience and his increasingly fruitful ministry, so far as their human qualities were concerned, were both an inheritance and an achievement; but always finally they were an achievement. He saw things through, and his mind was on the march.

Of course, I have gone far ahead of my story, but this is a rambling narrative that follows facts as they appear, or "leads" as they open.

When Clark reached his conclusion to be a preacher, to follow "the vicious circle," I do not know; but I am sure he had not been long there when he told me of his arrival. I had gone to Detroit in the pre-Easter season of 1931 to deliver a series of noonday addresses in a mid-city theater, and he came on from Hope College to spend an afternoon and night with me. I saw him enter the theater as I rose to speak. Afterward we went to lunch, saw a movie, and then I gave him a steak dinner—a big, juicy, thick steak with all the fixings. He was having a great deal of trouble with the wrist he had broken in the previous football season, and he was wearing a heavy leather guard. We saw a Detroit specialist together. It was apparent even then that his football days were over, for he was too light for any line position, and his strength to the team in both tackling and passing was now a thing of the past.

I thought that the painful wrist was responsible for his unusual silences. He did little talking until we retired. But then he began! We had a room with twin beds, with only a small night stand between us. It was late and I was ready to sleep, but he had just begun to talk. He spared neither subjects nor his tired father. Several times I was on the verge of telling him to shut up and go to sleep, but each time I stopped just on the verge and listened, for *something* was there—something unsaid after all the saying and, though I had no intimation of what it was, something that I knew instinctively I must wait to hear. Gradually he ran down, or seemed to, and at last he grew silent; but still I waited. Then it came. Quietly, but so impressively that as long as I live I shall remember the electric-like shock with which I heard him speak the words, he opened his boy heart, and I saw my son as in all the years before I had never known him. He flung his left arm with its sound wrist across my bed; I felt his hand over my chest and then I heard him say, "Daddy, I'm going to preach; I've got to do it!"

I wasn't sleepy and I wasn't tired then. Then I knew that always

I had *wanted* that, even when I was sure he would be the first lawyer of our line. And I had been delighted with the thought. But I think all fathers, whatever their worthy professions, have a sense of fulfillment, a subtle feeling of vindication, when a son follows after. The night approached another dawn before we went to sleep.

The next ten years—a little less than ten—were, I am sure, the best of Clark's less than thirty-three. "Best," I mean, by the tests of study, companionship, eager search for an adequate equipment for a great mission, and the glory of love with the opening of a prophetic ministry. Also Corky came along in those years—but here I refuse to run ahead of my story.

Only a few of the experiences of these years are written down here, but they are the major ones of which I have knowledge.

It was during Clark's first year at Yale that he and I took a walk down the abandoned ridge road toward High Pines, where a Governor of New Hampshire was born and where, at the time, an uncle and aunt were spending the summer. He had sent another telegram, this time from New Haven just to make sure that I would be at Long House. It read: "Most important. Must see you." At the time he was serving the South Meriden Methodist Church as a student pastor. He arrived at night and the next morning we took our walk—a walk, not a hike, for we were chiefly interested in undisturbed conversation.

He waited until we had crossed the main highway and climbed the long hill leading off to the right. We were in the deep, silent woods now, and he began to talk: "Dad, an old man is dying in my parish and he wants me to say something to him. He needs me, Dad, and I haven't anything to say."

We stopped by a stone wall and he waited. The words rang in my ears—"He needs me and I haven't anything to say." That was a large order, but at any rate the matter had been frankly stated. Clark was a very young minister and this was the first time Death had come to him.

I told him of my first time with Death—out in Ohio when the mother of six small children left them all weeping at her bed, the youngest sitting on the pillow by her head. But the principal thing was this: I told him that he must have something to say before he could say it and something to give before he could give it; and also that since he so greatly desired to be helpful, there was no question at all about receiving, that here the problem resolved itself into "Ask and ye shall receive"—that it was as simple, but as profound as that.

We talked to the heart of Life's mystery, its beginning and its end in Time, which we agreed was only the beginning. We agreed together there in the ancient colonial roadway that this life is the childhood of our immortality, and then we knelt together in the long dry grass among the dead leaves by the granite wall.

I left him and walked home alone. Later when he returned, I saw that he had the answer; I knew that he would not disappoint the dying man in South Meriden; that he was going back with something to say, something to give—something that in the short time of his ministry he said and gave to a great many people.

South Meriden was Clark's first real pulpit and parish responsibility; but two years before, he had served for a summer in the ancient village of Clinton Grove, which is only a few miles from Long House. Mrs. A. Ray Petty was his friend and church advisor. Mrs. Petty, the wife of one of the most distinguished of Baptist ministers and the mother of another who bears his father's name, was then director of the Deering Community Center with all its youth activities. She has written some deeply moving words about that summer: "Clark Poling endeared himself to the families of Deering and Clinton Grove, New Hampshire. He had been an important member of the younger groups before 1934, but that summer he became an outstanding person.

Deering Community Center invited him to become the leader of its staff of resident workers—young men and young women. The young people were enthusiastic about him, for Clark would ask no work of others in which he did not share. I remember one morning when I tried to find him for an important conference with Bishop Dallas and other religious leaders of New Hampshire. I hunted everywhere. At last I came upon him helping some of his boys clear large boulders from a road. Clark had taken off his shirt and was swinging a pick—doing the hardest part of the work. Slipping into his shirt and coat, he came in to lead the conference, taking part in the discussion with great helpfulness and understanding. He was equally at home working on the road as leading the discussion. The little village of Clinton Grove was without a minister and Clark was invited to preach. Services were held in an old Quaker school house, and the people came from miles around to hear him. How they loved him; How quickly he became a vital part of their community life! He was their pastor as well as their preacher. He called on their sick and listened to all their problems. The older people delighted in talking to him, and the young people made him their confidant and friend.

"There were many denominations represented in that little New England church—Quaker, Unitarian, Baptist, Methodist, Congregational, and Catholic—but presently all united under Clark's leadership. He preached the kind of Christ they needed and preached Him so simply and attractively that they accepted Him.

"Always the little village of Clinton Grove will bear the imprint of that summer with Clark."

But South Meriden gave Clark his first serious preaching experience, and he never ceased expressing his appreciation for that opportunity. Recently in New Haven I met the young man from Clark's South Meriden Church who is now finishing his course at Yale Divinity. Speaking of those days and of Clark, he said,

"I am here, you know, because of your son—he did it!" And then he turned quickly away.

From South Meriden he was called to be the student assistant in the First Church of Christ, the old parish church of New London, Connecticut, and for three years he had a radiant, fruitful ministry in association with the senior pastor, James Romeyn Danforth, also a Yale Divinity School man and a most gracious personality. The Danforth home, with Mrs. Danforth to give it friendly charm, was always open to him.

The New London years were crowded with enriching experience in study and friendship, as well as in parish activities, in preaching, in visitation, and especially in work with children and young people. Clark's junior church was perhaps the pioneer in its distinctive field, and I do not believe there has ever been one more successful. Also he wrote and directed a number of plays and pageants that evidenced maturing talent. I am glad these are preserved. Perhaps they may even be published—I am of the opinion that they merit many another presentation. While he was in New London, he became interested in youthful delinquents. Co-operating with the city authorities in a number of special cases, he showed a definite understanding of the personal situations involved, as well as an ability to deal constructively with the cases assigned him. He taught Bible classes at the Connecticut College for Women and gave a good deal of his time to state Christian Endeavor activities and to youth programs in other churches than his own.

Yes, New London days were days of growth in the life of our son. Aside from his ordination service and a few—all too few—personal visits, I had little direct association with his New London ministry, but I was increasingly grateful for his deepening note of assurance and power. Perhaps *power* is not the word, for gentleness distinguished his ministry; but what I found was surely power, too.

And speaking of gentleness, a little old woman, long from Scotland and quite alone, was his landlady. She was a pensioner of the church and a blessed soul, but her house, heavily mortgaged, was anything but comfortable—in fact, I was greatly disturbed over the physical conditions under which our son lived. But there was no moving him! He adopted the little lady and never ceased looking after her until in his early Schenectady days he returned to New London and tucked her wasted body under the sod. Yes, he was like that and couldn't be changed.

It had been increasingly apparent that Clark was ready now for his own church, for a ministry in which he would be responsible for the complete direction of a parish; and when one Thursday afternoon I dropped off a Boston train to spend a few hours with him before going on to New York, he was considering a possible survey visit to a church and community in the Middle West. We had a long talk at the supper table and then returned to his room, where we found a special delivery letter awaiting him, postmarked "Schenectady." Yes, that was the letter. Oh, the letter itself was merely an invitation for him to supply the pulpit of the First Reformed Church (Dutch) in Schenectady on the ensuing Sunday, but he and I both felt that in it was the voice of destiny— though we were properly reticent about saying so. We talked about Schenectady until my train pulled into the station.

Clark was very proud of his early Dutch Church associations in New York City. Always, whatever his immediate relationship, he felt himself to be a son of the Reformed Church in America; and he was proud, too, of the Dutch blood in his veins. All of this prejudiced him at once in favor of Schenectady—should he ever have the chance to consider the old First Church. Well, that chance came to him. So happily impressed was the congregation by his first and only appearance in the pulpit after the committee's invitation was extended, that a special meeting of the congregation was called for the following Friday night and unanimously he was called as the pastor. Immediately arrangements were made for his early installation.

On the program were his intimate friend, Rev. Howard J. Conn, his brother Daniel, Rev. J. Romeyn Danforth of New London, and the President of the Schenectady Classis of the Reformed Church in America, Rev. Gerard R. Gnade. I preached the installation sermon.

Schenectady

Of course, I cannot write of Clark's Schenectady ministry as perhaps it should be told; for though I was not there in person, I am too close to it, too intimately related to the young minister! The generous words of his friends and associates are the better telling of the story, and for that reason I have gathered some of their words together for this little volume.

My own visits when I came with Clark's mother were great occasions in our lives, and the coming of Corky's "Pretty Mummie Betty" so quickly to stand by the side of our son in the Schenectady parish (though on the date of his installation she was still the lovely Elizabeth Jung of Philadelphia) added greatly to the happiness of these events. During the installation service she sat demurely in her pew, the young minister's affianced bride, upon whom all eyes—covertly at least—were fixed. What they saw was much to their satisfaction.

I well remember our first visit to the small apartment and our walk by the river, our reading of the historical markers in the streets, our intimate study of all the symbolic architectural features of the beautiful church building, and our visits in the homes of the congregation. How enthusiastic Clark was with an enthusiasm that never lessened and that, when he made his last round of never-to-be-forgotten parish calls, was still a rising tide. He reveled in the great traditions of Church, of College, and of the City;

he gloried in the past and dreamed his dreams of an even greater future. Each subsequent visit added to our wealth of knowledge and increased our own enthusiasm as Clark told his story.

For him the most sacred spot in the Church was the tower room under the spire, where the stained-glass windows tell the story of the death of the first pastor of the church. This young Dominie Peiter Tasse Macher was killed and scalped in the French and Indian massacre of February 8, 1690, when the little stockade settlement was destroyed. Peiter Tasse Macher was also the first Protestant clergyman to be ordained in the New World, and Clark had a plan to build in that tower room under the beautiful spire a chapel for the worship of all people. That would be for the youthful martyr a worthy memorial, and it would become presently a shrine of inter-faith significance.

I watched with ever increasing pride the development of qualities of leadership within our son's mind and spirit. His program for children and youths, under the guidance of Dr. Ernest Ligon of Union College, was one of the most practical and impressive in America; his plan of evangelism broke out into new and neglected areas—neglected, perhaps, because generally not thought of at all. In these areas he reached men who had long remained indifferent to organized religion. Clark did not have the restless feet of some of his immediate forbears; he was constantly and intensely engaged with the church and her varied mounting activities. I am sure the generous appraisal of those who have written the intimate story of his Schenectady ministry is justified and true, and that already he had become a man for the hour with the full and radiant promise of yet greater things—when World War II interrupted his plans and changed his schedules. Of all this we shall write in the two final portions of our story. . . .

But I have reserved for just this place the finest and to me the most poignant experience of Clark's approach to his high calling. Already he had made his decision, and the experience itself came after our night together in Detroit; but it is significant of a search that never ceased and of a mysticism that deepened with the years. As to the search, Clark was never a man to write "finally" after any personal religious experience or decision. His was never the pose of "I have it all." Before he married Betty, he told her that, though he did not anticipate any change, if ever he should discover himself mistaken and a misfit in the pulpit, he would resign the ministry. Schenectady gave him the final word on that; and when he donned the chaplain's uniform, any question about the validity of his call and choice were behind him. In one of his later letters he wrote that he had just one desire: to get through with the war experience, to finish that job and then get back to his life's work in Schenectady—and to Corky's mother and to Corky and to "Thumper."

The experience is forever associated with Long House and, more than any granite ledge, it is the crown of what was then Wolf Hill.

One August afternoon Clark came to me and said, "Dad, I'm going up to Wolf Hill tonight after dinner, and I'll not be back— well, for some time. I'm taking a blanket and a canteen and please, Dad, don't worry about me and keep Mother from worrying. My return is indefinite." And he grinned. "I may stay twenty-four hours or longer, but there are some things I want to settle, Dad, and I hope I won't be interrupted. I wouldn't have said anything, but all of you would have been anxious about me. Of course, you'll understand—and help me?"

Well, I wasn't sure I understood, but I knew that I should help him and I tried to.

Off he went after the evening meal, with his blanket and canteen; but he resolutely rejected the suggestion that he take at least a few sandwiches. The night was clear and filled with stars, with no moon until early in the morning. The day that followed was one of New England's finest, and again the night was ex-

uisitely beautiful, but by three o'clock the next morning I had
eached the end of waiting. Our mother had for hours been re-
iinding me of the ledges and of the sheer drop on the west side
f Wolf Hill—a precipice she had never seen, but which loses
othing in some descriptions. Clark had been gone nearly thirty-
x hours and no sign had come back.

I could wait no longer. Just as the moon broke out of the
orizon, I took the south road with Fluff at my side. Foxes paral-
led us left and right, back a hundred yards or so from the road
nd barking in staccato yelps. But Fluff gave them no attention—
ie had learned the futility of excitement. We came to the Ells-
orth line wall in a jog, and then started the direct climb to the
ummit. Without the moon, soon even the dog would have been
 trouble. And now my anxiety took on proportions.

"Why had I waited? Of course, he did not mean *two* nights—
tterly foolish. I had been derelict. Mother was right. He could
ave broken a leg that first evening. Cold up there, too; one
lanket, one canteen—and he drinks like a fish. No food. What
 fool I've been! God help . . ." And so, as in all similar situa-
ons (though never had my fatherhood known another such
me), I came to prayer.

Some climb it was! Even Clark never made it more quickly,
am sure. I ran myself nearly blind before I reached the last pitch.
stopped then to breathe, to catch up in breathing, and with the
st of the long breaths I shouted our son's name, which is Corky's
me. "Clark!" Shouted it at the top of my voice, shouted it with
mething akin to terror, terror and remorse. There was no answer,
 reply. Fluff stood quietly at my side; even she had caught
 familiar scent. And then I did climb! That last pitch was done
 less than nothing, I am sure; and at every step, with every
ride, I shouted, "Clark!"

Parenthood is a strange, a mysterious experience. Only mother-
od reaches its final heights and depths, but fatherhood, too, can

be profound and poignant. That night on the summit of Wo
Hill under a midsummer moon, for one man fatherhood w
infinite anguish.

Then out of a crevice, where some day Clark's children sha
play, rose a tousle-headed lad. Startled from his sleep, he stoc
for an instant uncertain of his surroundings; and then in a voi
that always I shall hear, he said, "Dad!" and came to meet m
No other time had ever been like that, and never could there
another just like it.

We did not linger there but came quickly down the trail. Flu
leaped and yelped about the boy, expressing all that I could on
feel; and he, after our first greeting, was silent until we reach
the road. He talked then. He was glad I had come; but glad, to
that I had not come before. "I had some things to settle," he sai
"and I thought that up there I might hear The Voice. I did n
hear it—not The Voice," he continued. He spoke very slowly a
as though only incidentally to me. "But, Dad, I am glad I wer
yes, I'm glad. Some things are clearer now and other things w
be, I know." And I knew that on the mountain he had m
himself.

In those last words Clark was his buoyant self again. "G
Daddy, I'm glad you came up," he said and swung close to r
until, as so often they did when we tramped, our should
touched. "Is Mother worried?" His voice was penitent. "Brea
fast will sure taste good." And now we were back to earth.

Wolf Hill was to Clark what in Bible times the ancient peo
called "The Mount of Sacrifice," where they went to meet th
God. Now it bears another name and has, for all faiths and rac
an even braver message than ever its signal fires flashed across t
Contoocook valley when first the settlers came.

PRETTY MUMMIE BETTY

WHEN Billie, Clark's youngest sister, and I first saw the girl who was to become Corky's "Pretty Mummie Betty," it was for us love at first sight. "Oh Daddy," Billie said, "I wish that Clark could meet her!" It was in the fall of 1936 and the family, or what was left of it, our mother, Jane, Billie, and I, had moved to Philadelphia where I had become minister of Baptist Temple, the church of Russell H. Conwell, who was the founder of Temple University (named after the church).

On one of our first days in the city of "Brotherly Love," a professor of the University, who was also faculty advisor of the Student Christian Association, came to the church study with the president of the Association to invite me to speak to the students. And Elizabeth Jung, daughter of Rev. August Jung, a Presbyterian clergyman (Corky's other grandfather, with whom he celebrates a common birthday on September 15), was the president of that student group. Well, what our enthusiastic daughter Billie said about Miss Elizabeth Jung expressed exactly what I felt. I can see her now just as we saw her then—lovely, gracious, and with an infectious quality of charm.

That first visit was followed by others. Betty Jung took Jane and Billie under her wing and gave them many introductions to Philadelphia. Several times she was a visitor in our home; and on one occasion when she came to the church study, I showed her family pictures for the simple purpose of giving her an eyeful of the young man who was destined to become her husband. Well, she was politely interested, of course; but to be quite truthful I felt a little foolish after she was gone. And parents should feel that way when they mix too much in matters such as these. Of course, even parents have eyes and ears and—preferences.

We had lived in Philadelphia for nearly two years before Billie had her first real chance to introduce her brother Clark to Betty. She made one valiant effort that resulted in a humiliating anti-climax for her. A party arranged for Clark on the occasion of one of his hurried visits from Yale was set up for the one and only purpose of bringing the two together. There were others present, of course, but the rest just didn't count so far as Billie was concerned, though they did save her face when her recalcitrant brother developed a violent headache and spent most of that eventful evening upstairs.

Billie stormed all over him in the morning. "Why you villain!" she cried at the breakfast table. "You never had a headache in your life before. You've had everything else, but never that. And it was the nicest party of my life with the nicest girl you ever had a chance to meet and—"

Clark rumpled her up a bit and said, "There, there, little girl! Don't you cry. Didn't I take a car full of them home? Now which was this er—uh—?"

And then his youngest sister did explode.

She was to learn later that he had not been as blind as he professed nor as indifferent as he appeared. But there were only a few meetings between Betty and Clark before their precipitous courtship began. Of course, the families were becoming well acquainted in the meantime; and on several occasions, after some student function at the church or University, Betty was convoyed to her home in the Presbyterian manse on North 19th Street in the Poling car.

Once Jane met her at a Saturday night student affair in New York City, and later they found themselves together on the train returning to Philadelphia. That happened to be the week end of Clark's memorable visit when on Sunday night he preached in my pulpit. Among those in his congregation was a certain Miss Elizabeth Jung! But there came a day very soon thereafter when things really began to happen. I was quite set up when early one morning Clark put in his appearance quite unexpectedly, having taken the through-train from New London. To our mother I ventured the comment, "He's just a little homesick, I think." But shortly after breakfast while we were driving toward the church, I discovered my error.

"Dad," he said, and cleared his throat, "Dad," he repeated, "do you suppose I could reach Betty Jung? I might stay over and take her to a show," he concluded rather self-consciously.

"Betty? Betty who?" an old hypocrite replied. (Yes, I said "who.")

Clark snorted, "You know darn well *who*! Betty *Jung*, I said!"

I told him that I was sure her father had a telephone, but that I was pretty sure she would be "engaged"—that I knew she was very busy, but that he was welcome to use the "facilities of my study" to check up on the young woman.

He did, and strangely enough discovered that the very busy and very popular young lady just happened to have an open evening. Confidentially Betty afterward confessed that that evening was open only because she "re-opened" it!

As I remember it all now, that particular visit of Clark's came late in February or early in March, 1938, and the days immediately following found our second son spending much of his time either writing or riding to Philadelphia. Then came March 31. Our family will never forget that date. Of course the evening of March 31 merges into the dawn of April 1, but for obvious reasons we always celebrate the last day of March and not the first day of April.

Clark Vandersall Poling spent a good deal of time getting ready to go out that night; and after he went, he was gone a long time. Indeed when finally he returned, the house was locked in sleep— save for Billie, who was "psychic" in such matters. She was at the front door very soon after the bell "went off." Yes it went off, blew up, exploded, and until an electrician had been called, it never functioned again. There was an elevator in that old house— an elevator that Corky loved as a baby, but that he will not remember. Into it now came a shouting young man, madly swinging his sister and telling the world in general and his parents in particular that he was engaged! His voice was never less musical, but never more effective! By the time he reached our room, we had all the particulars; but even so, he raved on for another hour— not less than that. (How I wish that he could break in on our slumbers again, break into our chamber, with so glad a shout!)

Long before Clark finished his story that night, long before he had quieted down sufficiently to go on to bed, two of his most loyal friends and partisans, "Aunt Tillie and Aunt Lou," had been roused from their sleep and dragged from their beds. These sisters of our mother have been always of our home and clan and especially a living part of Long House. They had known Clark and loved him from the time when he began to ask his unanswerable questions. They had baked cakes for his hurried vacations and covered his retreat after many a boyhood escapade. And never did he cease to admire and love them.

No man was ever happier than Clark and no man ever surer that he had found the one woman in all the world and in all of time for him. That conviction never lost its radiance—the radiance of his engagement night. Indeed the joy that came to him when Betty Jung gave him her promise was so deeply moving as he shared it with those he loved that always they will treasure its memory and recall how it grew and deepened. That engagement was something! Certainly it was brief; they were married on June 21, less than three months after the wild last night of March.

But however brief, it was long enough for all parties concerned, and I know that to Clark it seemed an eternity.

The girl he was to marry was in herself resourceful and sufficient, and her home had given her a rare background of preparation and training. She, too, came from a large family, three sisters and three brothers. Her preacher father, whom Corky adores, is a noble man, and never was there a nobler woman than her mother. How the arrangements for the great day were so completely made in so short a time, I would never know; but they were made and the pictures of the happy occasion reveal something of the perfection with which Betty and her family planned that wedding day.

In the meantime Clark was spending a good many of his nights driving madly back and forth between Schenectady and Philadelphia. (He was already the newly installed minister of the First Reformed Church of Schenectady.) I am very sure that he drove too fast, too far, and too often; but for him, then as always, harder than working or serving—whatever the task—was waiting. And also—he was very much in love.

They were married in the church of the bride's father and by Rev. Jung, of course. I assisted. There was a lovely matron of honor and Daniel was best man. For once the elder brother's decorum was perfect, and he produced the ring at the right time and without visible effort. The two family pictures are interesting. There really had to be two because of the size of each family. But the very nicest picture is of Corky's "Pretty Mummie Betty" and her husband, snapped by a newspaper photographer just as they were ready to be driven away.

Clark's sister Ann, who knew and understood him so well, has written me this reminder of his wedding day: "Do you remember how he came down stairs that morning all dressed and ready to go to the church? Ascot correctly tied, gloves on, even the ring in his hand ready for the best man—he was all that a correct bridegroom should be. And then you noticed that he had forgotten to shave! He shaved and arrived at the church a little breathless, but intact and on time! That was Clark—he always got there, but frequently he was a little breathless." And then Ann added: "In any crucial test Clark always made out, always delivered the goods."

There was a brief honeymoon at Lake Mohonk and then the young "Dominie" brought his bride to their first Schenectady home, and in that small apartment began the five golden years of their life and ministry together. It is good to remember how truly it was "their ministry together"; no person of that congregation ever thinks of one without remembering the other. Theirs was a beautiful and complete human partnership, and they were radiantly one of another. Their first quarters were small, but large enough to receive their friends and young people particularly— the "unattached" of the General Electric Company especially were always about.

Clark lived in his congregation and preached out of its hunger and need. His visits were never forgotten and his deepening love for people became steadily more mature and understanding. I have written elsewhere of his parish planning and of his program for youth. The officials of the church have said of his brief pastorate that it was successful beyond all that even the most sanguine of his parishioners had hoped. They have written: "When Clark Poling came to the First Reformed Church, the average attendance at a regular service was thirty-five and there were only fifteen children in the Sunday school. He accepted leadership when the church was most inactive. His untiring efforts, his outstanding character and his devotion, in five years rebuilt this church until it is now one of the most active religious centers in the community. . . . He left to serve his country, but that was not the sole purpose of his leaving—also he went that he might better serve his church and community when he returned."

In writing to me of Clark, Mayor Mills Ten Eyck of Schenectady said: "He was richly endowed in mind and spirit. A gentleman by instinct. . . . He was one of those who loved his fellow men. He gave his life for something that outlasts life."

Dr. Burges Johnson of Union College tells of how Clark persuaded Mrs. Johnson and him to unite with the church: "I was not a member of any church in Schenectady. When we came here, we found a regular service at the college chapel and we felt that attendance there was important. But we wanted to be connected with some local congregation and contribute to the support of an organized church in the community. My acquaintance with your son led me to choose his church. He made several efforts to get me to unite and we argued a good many theological questions when he made his parish calls.

"I delighted in his earnestness, his sincerity, and the consistency of his daily living with his beliefs.

"We were both directors of the Schenectady Boys' Club, and during my presidency I found that I could always depend upon him to accept any sort of responsibility and then attend to it promptly and efficiently. He did not take on any social obligation in the community without giving it devoted service, and I marveled that he found time enough for all of his community work. . . . It is hard to convey in exact words the relationship between Clark and myself, and my affection for him."

One incident of Clark's Schenectady ministry took place in Wheeling, West Virginia, and of it Daniel writes: "The experiences my brother and I shared were many. The one that lingers in memory now is Wheeling, West Virginia, May 31, 1940, where he came and helped install me as minister of the First Presbyterian Church. Arriving in the morning, my father and I met him at the station. I recall the difficulties he encountered in reaching Wheeling from Schenectady, and what he had to say about them! The day was especially happy. The birds were everywhere and the rambler roses, in almost every yard, were in full bloom. It meant so much to us to have my mother, who had come with my father, and my brother in our new home. The service of installation commenced at 7:45. A fine congregation assembled to witness the installation of the new minister by his father and younger brother. My brother's part was the charge to the minister, a major portion of the program. All were interested to hear him and eagerly awaited his time to speak. When his turn came, none were disappointed. I see him now. In his black robe he took his place at the right of the pulpit and opened his address with these words: 'For years my brother, being older, has "charged" me. He has never spared himself in this responsibility. Now that the tables are turned and my time has come, I intend to give back full measure.'

"He won the congregation, of course, and they hung on every word of his unusual and well-prepared message. My brother 'stole the show'! Many times in my brief three-and-a-quarter years' ministry in that great old Wheeling church, his name was mentioned. Although I may be soon forgotten, the "charge" he gave to me that night will always be remembered."

Of course, it is quite impossible in any letter, however long, to tell the story of Clark's and Betty's five years together in Schenectady, but Betty has written me these intimate paragraphs that Corky and Susan will always be glad to have:

"Here are some little snatches from my memories of our Schenectady days together:

"Clark's 6 A.M. tennis matches with some of the men of the church.

"The three- and four-day combination conference and camping trips to Mt. Marcy with young people's groups. Clark's idea was to make your religion hard. So we hiked for a whole day. Hiked up the mountain to the summit where we pondered the wonders

of God's world, if we could stop thinking of our aching legs! Then
he and I cooked food for sixteen or twenty starved youngsters,
after which we swatted Adirondack 'punkies' for the rest of the
night. Incidentally we all carried packs filled with provisions and
camping equipment.

"Our 'squeezed in' shows, after a meeting. Movies were Clark's
chief joy and relaxation. Light movies, and the 'funnies.'

"His traditional and open dislike for liquor and tobacco! He'd
chide the women for their 'wicked habit,' cigarettes! But he did it
in such a way that they 'loved it.'

"One incident always stood out in Clark's mind as just about
the 'funniest'—on himself. He was conducting funeral services
for a ninety-year-old lady whom everyone called 'Grandmother' or
'Mother Van Vost.' In the course of the service, he spoke of her
children and her grandchildren loving and respecting her. Instantly
he realized that the dear old lady was a spinster, and he saw one
of the front-row mourners nudge her neighbor and smile. Quickly
he got himself in hand and did it so well that many thought he
had made no mistake, but intended to pay the deceased a high
compliment by referring to her unselfish love of others, who were
as her very own children and grandchildren. Well, it taught him
one lesson. He never again gave 'funeral orations' in such a personal manner. Clark admitted to me that he had a hard time
getting through the rest of that service fast enough. He just had
to get outside and laugh—that nervous laugh of his.

"Yes, and he was absent-minded. He might look for his car a
whole day before remembering that he had left it at a garage for
repairs. Always I would know that something was wrong and I
might ask, 'Is it the car?'

"He left one father of a bride standing at the bride's side
throughout the entire ceremony, waiting for his cue to say, 'I, her
father.' (*Note:* So did his dad!)

"Several times he forgot to tell me about guests he had invited for dinner, and on one occasion he forgot so completely that when he saw the gentleman headed in the direction of our house, my absent-minded husband stopped the car and asked our prospective guest where he was going! Well, the shock he received when he got the man's answer was no greater than mine when they both appeared. I had just one portion of liver—for I detest liver. I entertained the guest while Clark went out for more liver. He came back with steak, to the satisfaction of the guest, who later confessed that his heart and stomach both sank when he heard the word. He also detested liver.

"Was ever a man as constantly generous, both wisely and unwisely, as Clark? For the first year of our married life we 'paid off' on a typewriter that Clark bought from a boy who was just starting out as a salesman. To give the lad a '*good* start,' Clark ordered the best, the most expensive machine in the catalogue, even though he couldn't type and had no intention of learning. Well, 'good start' or not for the boy, it proved to be quite a 'back set' for us.

"When Corky arrived, we were fortunate in having both a housekeeper and a nurse. The second day that I was allowed to be up and about, the nurse left for another case; also Clark 'loaned' the housekeeper to a family in which both children and mother were sick. I was swamped. Weak from more than a month in bed, I found myself in the midst of a brand new situation with my first baby—his formula to make up, his diapers to wash, and the hundred other baby things to do, to say nothing of feeding the baby's father and getting the house in order. But what a 'mother's helper' Clark was! He joined me in everything and never ceased being interested in all the details.

"Do you remember the pledges he made to organizations and institutions which I seldom got to know anything about? He would give the 'shirt off his back,' and actually I've argued with him to prevent him from giving away his other pair of shoes or his extra pair of trousers! 'Why should any man have two when another has none?' he would say.

"We had regular visits from certain 'gentlemen of leisure'—non-enforced leisure—who knew where they could get a good meal. Clark rarely gave them money, but he had an arrangement with a restaurant in the neighborhood where a man was given a full dinner upon presenting Clark's card.

"There were little details that Clark couldn't always master, and some of these gave us both a lot of fun—also anxiety. One was his inability to memorize verbatim. Many a Sunday morning I would 'sweat' through a four-line poem while he staggered on to an unrhythmic or unrhyming end! Even now I find myself 'sweating' whenever a minister launches into verses. I hold my breath until he's through.

"As to names, often he would ask me out of the side of his mouth 'Who is she?' or 'What's his name?' It was almost unforgivable if I didn't 'come through.' You see that was part of my job. And how wonderful it was! How glorious beyond words!

"Wherever I go, always Schenectady will be a part of me. Never was anyone happier than I. My family were a bit hurt, I fear, because I never was homesick. How could I be? Clark filled every moment of my married life and I was completely content.

"He had carefully thought through just what marriage should be for both parties, and outside of his work—which was his 'first love'—I was always his chief concern. His desires, his wants, his comforts were last.

"Two things, as I look back, were the basis of our happiness. First, our love for each other and our desire to do everything possible each to make the other happy. Second, our love for Christ, His church, and the work of His Kingdom—perhaps the order should be reversed. I knew that Clark's 'call' was the most important thing in our lives, and that all other matters were secondary to that. Oh, yes, I was impatient at times when I didn't see all of him that I wanted, but basically what I have written is true. Always I counted it my highest privilege to share in Clark's work. The lot of a minister's wife has often been compared to that of a doctor's, but I fail to see the comparison. A doctor's wife can never share her husband's work directly (unless she is actively his assistant). A minister's wife may. Because of this so much was added to our living, in those four Schenectady years. Certainly I saw more of Clark than many other wives see of their husbands—even if it was across the church. But just that was enough for me.

"It is rather hard to think now of special incidents. There are so many things to tell. Oh, I want all of you to appreciate and to know Clark as only I could have known him in those years before he went off to the war.

"What joy he experienced after calling on his parishioners— what happiness when he baptized children and married young people. Particularly the latter, for he used to say that he was happy knowing what happiness was in store for them—and how carefully he'd discuss with each couple the forthcoming step with all its hidden factors. He had satisfaction with big jobs well done, but there was joy, too, over details such as church calendars. With infinite care he worked out every detail—choosing the paper, selecting the type. Everything had to be done right or he'd have none of it!

"Being an idealist, he was very particular about certain details. You remember the matter of wedding fees. He never took money for his weddings—you know why. To be sure it wasn't because it was never offered! Although he'd explain very carefully to every couple his feeling on the matter, the envelope was nevertheless offered. There were several things he would do then: sometimes he would give the envelope to the bride; sometimes he'd encourage the couple to make a special gift to a charity or benevolent cause; or he might put the money into a special fund (along with money from funerals) which he used for extra printing, such as special calendars, booklets, pictures of the church, etc. This enabled him to do many interesting and unexpected things for people. Now the wedding fees belong traditionally to the minister's wife, as you know. Well, he gave me all his honorariums from outside speeches. Almost without exception, we used this money for special trips or "treats." To my mind these were some of our most wonderful experiences together. And I financed them!

"More about the weddings: In his discussions with the young couples, he asked three things of them: that they find a church home, not necessarily ours, and that they attend regularly; that they resolve to bring up their children in the church; and that in case of marital difficulty they consult with him before they reached a major decision.

"Always Clark was on the go. Almost as soon as he reached Schenectady he got into civic affairs, and the Boys' Club was one of his greatest interests. The Club was located near the church. Clark felt that the church had a direct responsibility to the community in which it was located—the community being largely made up of others than those who were members of the congregation. It was his deep desire and greatest dream that eventually his church would serve the community in a significant way. Now I know that his dream will come true."

Speaking of Clark and that dream, Dr. Ernest Ligon, Associate Professor of Psychology at Union College, with whom Clark worked so closely in the Character Research Project, has said, "Clark came to Schenectady and in five years transformed a church that was virtually dead into one that was fast becoming the most influential in the community. And in his death left so great an influence that his church has not hesitated to set forth on a highly ambitious church school project as a memorial. Even in his death he is intensely alive." (Dr. Ligon's complete letter appears in the Postscript.

I have reserved this place for the letter written to me by the distinguished president of Union College, Dixon Ryan Fox: "Clark Poling will mean much permanently in the memory of Schenectady. He brought to his pastorate here a wisely disciplined energy and a boundless and buoyant faith in the power of religion among men and women. His serene good temper, his instant sympathy, and his anxiety to help made him an ideal pastor. His unfailing personal poise was always a reassurance in any gathering, and his obvious learning, even though modestly revealed, stimulated the good ambition of others. I know that many young lads in Schenectady took him as a model and his example, sealed with his final heroism, will remain with them.

"We were proud to have his annual participation in our Founders' Day ceremonies at Union College, for in official descent he represented our academic founder, the Reverend Dr. Dirck Romeyn, pastor of his church in the seventeen-nineties. It was an inspiration to hear him read the scripture, and even to see him walk across the chancel—seeming, at least, to be the perfectly adjusted man. What times I had opportunity to hear him preach I much enjoyed, for he always paid us the compliment of thorough preparation and had something valuable to say. I know that he drew to his church many who had not previously been given to regular church worship. We are very grateful to the choice that brought him to us—to leave so much behind."

That Clark never lost his intimate touch with the Schenectady Church and never ceased from longing to return is made clear in a series of letters to his intimate friend, Rev. Franklin G. Hincamp. Rev. Hincamp had been assigned by the Classis of Schenectady responsibility for the spiritual guidance of the congregation during the young pastor's absence. In one letter Clark wrote: "If anyone should ask, you tell them I would almost go AWOL to see Betty and the Church! Army life is interesting but, Franklin, it is not normal, and for its own sake I do not like it. Always a minister is lonely in a sense, but in a normal set-up he has his family. As for the chaplains, they are fine men on the whole, and they have the opportunity to do—and definitely are doing—a good job. Yes, they are a superior group, but the uniform does not change the heart of a man—only the love of Christ does that. . . . The enlisted men and the selectees exhibit the strength and weakness of men everywhere. I like them. I get along with them. I am confident that with equipment and leadership the enlisted men will meet and defeat the enemy and their own personal fears. . . .

"Naturally I was troubled by a good many things that I saw. Particularly I appreciated the quality and character of officers trained at West Point. The Regular Army and the West Point graduates are better disciplined; they are gentlemen, too. My recipe for a good army is compulsory military training for every male and the enlarging of West Point and Virginia Military Institute! We need more 'school' and fewer political soldiers."

Again he wrote: "I have been treated mighty well. The men think well of the office of chaplain. They come to us frankly and treat us with respect and affection. I know that I can do good and I do not regret my decision to enter the Army. While I am lonely and miss the church more than I could ever anticipate, this was the only thing I could do, and it was right. God moves in many ways and I feel that it was intended for me to become a chaplain." He wrote concerning communion services; he wrote asking for the names of the sick; he wrote to those who had lost loved ones; he made suggestions for his consistory. In one letter he asked that above all he must not be considered personally in the matter of a resident pastor for the church, if and when the church began to suffer because of his absence.

Concerning the men and their spiritual interests, in one letter he said, "They want to know what to believe and how to act.

This seems to me of major significance because for years people in some circles have been saying 'it does not matter what you believe so long as you live a good life.' "

My final quotation from his letters to Rev. Hincamp refers to an anticipated furlough "sometime in November, unless we are out of the country, which is a very real possibility. If I do get back, I want to be able to preach; I want the consistory to hire a taxi and let me give three days to intensive calling. I am sure I can make at least sixty calls in three days. And finally I want two letters circulated through the church. I see that I have only twenty dollars left in my special fund (Betty has written of that!). Well, I shall solicit personally some more money and in this way finance the printing of the letters." In this same connection he writes, "My work becomes more and more absorbing, but I do get homesick for the church." And then again this note: "I could never have stayed out—I just had to do this." And this last word: "Each day that passes makes me more sure that the settled pastorate is the only place for me. Of course, when you are immersed in absorbing work you are happy, but I do want to get back soon!"

But when all is said, written, and done, Corky's arrival was the great event of Clark's four years in Schenectady. How eagerly he had looked forward to his first-born, and how concerned he was for the well-being of the baby's mother. He sent me back in memory to my own first experiences in fatherhood and fairly pumped me dry extracting information from which to take comfort and reassurance. "If anything happens to Betty," he declared fervently, "I'll never get over it and I'll never forgive myself." And he meant it, for when Corky was nested beneath his mother's heart, she was doubly precious to the man whose name the small boy carries.

As for her, she was more lovely than ever and even more constant in her poise and good spirits. Once she said, "Oh, don't worry, Clark. It won't be half as bad as that! I'll survive, and you'll make a good recovery, I know." And he did, and didn't we all!

Betty and Clark came to Long House several times that summer. The last time before the great event, they came in spite of the warning of the good doctor. Clark had been so eager to have Betty love Long House, and I think he was just a little fearful that having spent so many happy summers elsewhere she might not feel about his mountain just as he felt. But that summer of 1940 was her real introduction to Long House, and I think that her son must have come into the world with a prenatal affection for it.

I saw him first in the hospital when he was only a few hours old. Again I had returned from a journey when the birth message came. The voice of Clark was a triumphant shout on the telephone. Corky was *there*—his first-born, his son—and even more important to him, the mother was "all right." Well, Mother and I got down to Schenectady the next day and saw the baby first through the glass. An obliging nurse moved his crib close to the window, and that was as near as we got. I sniffed and remarked that I had been "right there when mine were born," but of course that was in a less scientific age. Corky had all the conveniences.

Clark was right at my shoulder and terribly anxious for me to get a good impression. "He's a little fellow, Dad, and they do look funny, don't they? But the doctor says he's perfect, perfect in every way, Dad, and Betty's wonderful. You've got to imagine him as he's going to be, Dad."

I shoved my hand through my son's arm and as we walked down to Betty's room together, I remembered, remembered well, another little red baby boy.

Corky's coming made many changes in his parents' plans and schedules. Almost immediately the little apartment which had grown too small was left behind, and the house—the only house Corky has ever known as home—came into his life. There I have seen him standing at the top of the long stairs, standing in his "birthday suit" and looking down through the railing; there I have watched him swinging under the great tree where his father lifted him; and there I have chased him through the garages at the rear, down toward the Mohawk River. He "shaved" with his daddy in the bathroom of that house and helped him with the furnace in the basement. In one direction beyond the "circle" is the store; and in the other, just around the corner, is the church; and from his first toddling hours Corky has been making both the store and church his destinations. Yes, he has been at times a "runaway"—in that he is like his uncle rather than his father and, simple honesty constrains me to add, more like the writer of these lines. But, of course, Corky's days with his daddy in the Schenectady house were not many—he was a very small lad when with his mother he was off to join his father in the Army camp. When he came back, it was different.

Corky had a little time with both his mother and father at Long House. Clark first brought him there. That made the young father very happy. I am sure that always he had looked forward to carrying his son into Long House even as he dreamed of the tramps they would have together down the lanes of Deering.

Corky spent one never-to-be-forgotten Christmas with his relatives in Philadelphia when he was just beyond his first birthday. He very properly divided time between his grandparents and at least once brought them all together in a gala celebration. In this same holiday season Corky met his great-grandfather Poling for the first time. My father had come on from Portland, Oregon. Corky also began his friendship with several of his cousins. He gave Phillips Wood, one sturdy cousin, quite the shock of his life when he proceeded to tear out the Dutch tile in the dining room. It was difficult for Clark to see in his son anything short of perfection, and of this fact Corky was already aware and governing himself accordingly. It was after this Christmas that Corky was baptized—baptized at the altar of his daddy's beautiful church. That was a unique service, for Corky's grandfather Jung, assisted by his great-grandfather Poling, was the officiating clergyman. Standing with Betty, Clark proudly held his son. Clark Vandersall Poling was the name they gave him—Clark Vandersall Poling, Jr.

CHAPLAINS COURAGEOUS

DURING the Christmas vacation just after Pearl Harbor, Clark talked to me about the chaplaincy and his decision to enlist. But there had been another conversation nearly a year before in which, with typical frankness, he had informed me that if we got into the war as he believed we would, he did not think that he would be satisfied to remain in civilian life, and he added, "But, Dad, if I go in, I'm not going as a chaplain!" And there was an unmistakable challenge in his voice.

We grinned at each other and then I replied, "Why? Are you afraid?"

That nettled him and he came back at me with an abrupt: "What do you mean by that?"

I knew that he was thinking of the more difficult and, as he regarded them, the more dangerous duties of armed conflict. He couldn't think of himself in a softer or more protected place than some other man, or of accepting a special consideration or exemption granted the ministry.

"Clark," I said, "you'll try to go in—if you go—where you can count for the most. That's first with you, I know; and in the second place, the chaplaincy had in the last war the highest casualty rate of all the services.*

---

* The mortality rate for chaplains [in World War I] was 1 out of 96—the highest for all Services. With regard to decorations for courage beyond the line of ordinary duty, 27 received the DSC, 5 the DSM, 57 were decorated by the United States Government, and 8 by foreign powers. The casualty record for chaplains in the present war is second only to that of officers in the Air Force. (See Nov. 17, 1941, issue of Time.)

He narrowed his eyes. "Are you sure of that, Dad?"

"Yes, I am sure. As a chaplain, you'll have the finest chance in the world to be killed. The only difference is this: you can't kill anyone. Along with the Medical Corps, you'll be unarmed."

We never discussed that phase of the matter again, and in our long talk just before Christmas, 1941, it was Clark's settled conviction that he should become a chaplain in the Army of the United States. Almost immediately he took action, informing his church of his purpose and making the necessary application. Then came weeks of waiting, and how impatient and concerned he was, fearing that he might be rejected.

To us as we look back upon those days, the time was all too short; and before we were prepared for the announcement, word came that his orders were ready; and we of the Philadelphia families were invited to attend farewell receptions and services in Schenectady. Corky was very much in evidence when we arrived and very much in his father's thinking. He had tremendous satisfaction in following his son's development, and he knew that he was going to miss the boy terribly.

Of all the affairs in those crowded days, I remember two especially: the farewell dinner in the Sunday school auditorium under the Christian Endeavor monogram, and the communion service that brought that evening to its unforgettable close. Clark made a simple, restrained, but deeply moving and eloquent speech. Of the speech Dr. Ernest Ligon wrote: "You had to see him at a dinner rise to such speaking heights as to outdo completely the guest of honor, his illustrious father." The "illustrious" is the only exaggeration in that sentence. The love of his church surrounded him that night and he was at his friendly, radiant best. He directed the communion, and never have I been more honored than I was as I stood with him at the altar he so greatly reverenced and with him ministered to the officers and members whom he so deeply loved. Mystic he was, though always a realist, too; but it was in blessing the emblems and in distributing to worshipers wherever they gathered that he came to the center and heart of his high calling.

There were still some weeks of waiting before he actually entrained for Camp Shelby in Mississippi; and until his very last day at home, he was the busy pastor of his church. But the formal farewells had now been spoken. Always we shall be happy to remember that his official relations to the Schenectady congregation were never broken or interrupted, for he was not allowed to resign. He was given leave of absence for the "duration" and continued to be the minister of the First Reformed Church until and beyond a certain dark February night in the North Atlantic. Yes, it was as minister of his church that he went into the chaplaincy of the Army of the United States, and for him that sacred relation continued through time and space unchanged and unbroken.

And now Corky's blessed mother has come to my help, for not one visit was I privileged to make to our son while he was in training. She has told me about her days with Corky and Clark at Camp Shelby in Mississippi, and at Miles Standish in Massachusetts—the training and waiting days before he sailed on his mission. At first he did not think that Betty and Corky could be with him, but his very first letter written from the South said that they simply *must* spend at least the month of August at the camp or near it. He made very careful plans for their visit—plans that began in those first twenty-four hours of loneliness after he left Schenectady. It was not easy for Betty to make the adjustment, for she was busy with the daily vacation school at the church, but presently they were there!

He met his little family at Gulfport, Mississippi. Corky was excited beyond belief. To his father he was perfect. His mother tells me that the way he talked, the way he was dressed, the very way he said "dada," was wonderful to the young chaplain, and that she could not disturb him at all by reminding him that

Corky was old enough to be saying whole sentences. And then it happened. Corky insisted on taking a doll into the dining room of the hotel! His father was horrified. He pleaded with his son and then commanded him, but the best he could accomplish was to convince the small boy that the doll was a boy and must now wear pants instead of dresses.

August days were hot and humid in Mississippi. The little apartment in which they settled was not the most comfortable spot in the world, but the three had a glorious time together. Breakfast was a family picnic, especially on the mornings when Clark's "ride" to the camp was late, and the small boy had another hour of play with the chaplain. Betty shared the family scene with boys from the camp, and there were few meals without four or five of them. But especially she looked forward to Sunday, for then the little family was together for the entire day. Corky went to the camp with his father and attended the services at the chapel; and often like the real minister's wife that she was, Betty played the organ. There would be dinner at the service club or the mess hall with the boys, for in this instance officers and enlisted men ate together.

August passed and September was well under way when came the first intimation of removal—the 131st QM had been "in" for two years now. Would Clark go? His only fear was that he might be left behind, and that was exactly what happened. He was transferred to the 501st Engineers, and Betty tells me that later he rather liked that, for, according to their own idea at least, they were the "fightin'est Engineers." But the heart of the young chaplain was heavy, for he had grown very much attached to his old outfit and he had so hoped to be with them in action. The boys, too, felt badly, for they had taken the chaplain into their lives. (Betty added here, "Who could resist him!") Then, too, he had been their very first chaplain.

One of the men of that outfit in an intimate letter from England wrote: "It is natural to seek an ideal. As long as I can remember, I have sought that reassurance and source of hope. I remember the day in June when he first came into the headquarters of the regiment and asked me what he should do about reporting to the commanding officer. I remember, too, how I cried and was hurt inside when I learned that he was not to accompany us; that he had been transferred. But his presence never left us. I felt it on the train. I felt it in the long weeks at Fort Dix, and crossing the ocean, and even now as I write, I feel it here in England. Always it will be this way. Not only for myself, but, believe me, for many of the men in this outfit. A week ago a commanding officer called us together and told us of the occurrence—about Clark—that he gave his life belt to another. He was that kind of person."

I have taken these lines from a letter written to Betty. There are some other sentences from a letter written to me by a cadet who was convalescing in the hospital at Camp Lee, Virginia: "I knew him for only four months while we were together at Camp Shelby—he exerted a profound influence in my life and in the lives of many others of the 131st. I recall many fine and thoughtful things he did for us boys. One very hot afternoon our detachment took a hike. It was led by a young lieutenant and at a tougher pace than any of us were prepared to go at that time. Your son was with us and at one stage was carrying two rifles for boys who needed to have their packs eased. I complained bitterly that night of the extra-rough workout, and I, with others, insisted that we did not have enough rest periods for such a hot day. Chaplain Poling said, 'Oh, you are just complaining.' But he made a round of the tents to check the condition of the boys, and when he came back to the office he said, 'Well, Horatio, you are right. It was too much of a hike. You and I are about the only ones who are able to get around. The rest are all flat on their backs in their bunks.' Then he went back to the tents and checked blisters and other ailments. Many times, sir, I recall the deep satisfaction he had in serving his first holy communion as an Army chaplain. How carefully he instructed those of us who were to assist him, in the significance of what we were doing together."

But the transfer to the 501st Engineers proved to be pleasant for Corky and his "Pretty Mummie Betty." She is sure that the happiest memory of Camp Shelby would be for Clark, as it is for her, the baptizing of his commanding officer's baby. It was a unique service in the Army chapel with the boys of all faiths attending, and with Clark in his clerical gown. But there continued to be uncertainty as to his future. He knew that when the 501st was moved out, he would very likely again be left behind; and so he wrote to the Chief of Chaplains, requesting a transfer to another combat unit and asking active duty for himself.

November, 1942, brought his orders. He managed then to give a few crowded days to Philadelphia and to home and church in Schenectady. How happy the three of them were on the long ride together!

There is another day Corky's mother remembers—the twenty-first day of November, when at five o'clock in the morning she said good-by to her husband for the second time. He was then on his way to his port of embarkation, and it looked like good-by for the duration; also Corky was a sick little boy. But at ten-thirty o'clock that same night the sun shone again! Clark telephoned and said that there would be some days of delay. "Will you come?" Betty tells me Clark asked.

"Would I? I fairly dragged Corky out of bed, but I did wait until I bought him a warm outfit—the change from the South to the North had been too much for the little fellow.

"On Wednesday we were ready, Corky was well enough, so off we went to Taunton, Massachusetts, and there in two rooms we spent the next two months. We had Thanksgiving and Christmas together and it was the happiest Christmas of our lives. Values do change, and we were so grateful just to be together. Life in

Taunton was much as it had been in Mississippi in one respect. We lived always with the anticipation of what the next moment would bring—something to part us for that undetermined time, the duration."

Corky's mother did not wish to return to Schenectady until Clark should be called out, but at last he took them both home, put the house in running order and, Betty says, "called on the sick and the aged in the congregation, held his last communion with his church officers—all in four days; and then on Thursday night, January 14, we said good-by at the train, fully expecting that the following week he would come home again."

But things moved more quickly. Tuesday he called to say that something was up. Wednesday: "It's a false alarm," and then Thursday Betty received a telegram: "Can't phone again. With my dearest love, Clark."

"So Corky and I settled back and waited for letters—we settled back not knowing just what life would be like without the man about whom our universe revolved. We were waiting for the day when he would come back, and the four of us (yes, the little one to be added) would take up life again, finishing to a happy ending what had had such a perfect beginning."

Corky's mother has told me many rollicking stories about him and his daddy in the camps. One had to do with Clark's G. I. shoes. One of Corky's favorite pastimes was to get into those shoes and walk up and down in front of the house in Hattiesburg. He was little and thin and the shoes were big and heavy for a tiny fellow, but when he was tired he just squatted on the backs of the shoes, for they came up to the level of a child's chair. Even now she can see her small son resting in the middle of the walk with his hands on his knees—resting and surveying his surroundings.

Clark never taught Corky to salute, but the boy was observing; and so presently when he saw his father returning the salute of the enlisted men, he saluted, too, solemnly and awkwardly, and at the first with his little finger pressed against his forehead. He learned quickly and soon saluted like a veteran.

In Gulfport one afternoon Corky almost upset Army discipline and civilian decorum. The uniform had made a deep impression, and at that time every uniform meant "Da-Da" to him. On this particular occasion, seeing a soldier and breaking away from his mother, Corky ran after the enlisted men shouting "Da-Da-Da," Betty pursued swiftly, telling her son that he was altogether mistaken. But Corky still clung to the tunic of the soldier. Finally the enlisted man turned to settle the matter once and for all. "You can't pin that on me!" he said.

They stopped in Philadelphia on their way to Schenectady from the South, and a grand time we all had together. Corky ran the elevator—at least he pressed the button and started it—and he had a thrilling experience running away in Broad Street. Once in Hattiesburg he had landed in the police station, where he entertained the officers until his family came for him.

Clark and I had our pictures taken together. We found an overcoat that made him look very much the soldier and chaplain, and we had long talks in the study.

One Wednesday evening he made a short address to the members of my church and told them that the Army would not "ruin" their boys. He said: "If your sons received good home training and example, if you taught them to pray and gave them the experience of the church, you may reasonably expect them to return as forthright as they were when they went away. The Army is a cross-section of America. Men do not become either saints or sinners just by putting on the uniform."

One evening Clark said to me: "Dad, you must be very considerate of Daniel. It is harder for him to stay than it is for me to go. It takes greater courage for him to do what he is doing than it does for me to do what I am doing." That was almost the last word that he had with me before he took Betty and Corky on to Schenectady. And I understood. Daniel had dreamed of the chaplaincy, too, and only stern duty kept him out. Each of these brothers was "loyal to the royal in himself," and that, of course, is a final test of true courage.

After our memorable times together in Philadelphia, I had one other day with Clark—with Clark and Betty and Corky together. They were then at Camp Miles Standish and came to Boston to meet me. They arrived early in the morning and we all ate breakfast together at the City Club. I must say that Corky's eating was nothing to brag about and he was all over the room and into everything. We visited the Headquarters Building of the World's Christian Endeavor Union; and when the lunch hour arrived, two of the young ladies took Corky along with them while Clark and I went out with Betty. That lunch of ours was really a major event, for we three had beautiful Martha Scott as our guest. Later we saw Martha, who is another member of our family's "wider fellowship," in her new play *The Willow*. That was an afternoon never to be forgotten. Good it is to remember, and in remembering to recall each little incident and many a phrase or word or "a look with word unspoken." We picked Corky up at the Christian Endeavor Building and later went to the Women's City Club for our family dinner. Corky was tired and gave his chaplain father an anxious thought or two, for he was always concerned that his son should be at his best in public, and perhaps also he feared that I might get a wrong impression. However, Betty kept things well in hand. I think that right here is just the place to insert Clark's letter to me in which he has a good deal to say about his son. It was written to his mother and me some days after our Boston visit together, and after he had sailed on his mission, but he had not forgotten one thing that I said that night in Boston!

"Dearest Dad and Mother:

"In order for you to check on whether my letters are getting through, I will number each one and you can keep a record. Mother's letter, which she gave to me in Philadelphia, slipped in with my orders, has been read, and is a very beautiful letter. . . .

"So far I have stood up pretty well against the sharp arrows of loneliness. I miss Betty and Corky terribly and I find myself turning unconsciously as though to tell Betty something. It is not so much the physical side of marriage that counts, as the constant comradeship with all the taken-for-granted little details of living together that makes for happiness.

"Corky is often in my mind. I have dreamed about him several times. The worse pangs come when I realize that he won't know me when I get back, and that he will be quite a different small boy. Dad made the remark that Corky might be better without me during these formative months! He must have been joking because I really have not spoiled him more than Betty. You must remember that you have seen him under most unfavorable conditions, hurried glimpses when Corky has been tired and in strange and difficult surroundings. I like to think Corky would benefit by having me to tell him stories and play with him.

"Incidentally, Corky loves stories. The last night I was at home he fell out of bed. We had given his bed to a little boy of some Army people who needed a place for a few days, so Corky was was in the big bed across the hall. He was very much disturbed and frightened by the sudden bump. But he wasn't too tired to want a story. 'Me tory' is what he says when he wants a story, and so I had to tell and retell 'Little Black Sambo.' Several times I dozed off but Cork would wiggle and say, 'Read me. Me tory,' and wake me up; finally we both went to sleep. And when eventually I woke up, there he was, a warm ball against my side clutching his 'book' tightly in one hand.

"Sometime I am going to start a 'David and Abram' series

of my own. Of course, the author will not be quite the frontiersman and big game hunter that the originator of the series was, but Corky won't know the difference unless you put something over on me, Dad. (Do you remember the hunting in Alaska? We certainly loved those stories. You will never have a more appreciative audience.)

"Did I tell you that Corky has now graduated from the 'Amen' limit to the repeating stage and can go through the entire length of 'Now I Lay Me Down to Sleep?' Also he can navigate through the various 'bless the relatives' all by himself. He even made a responsive reading out of 'Now I Lay Me,' for he would continue by himself 'Down to Sleep.' Pretty good for a boy not two and a half years old! I love you both,

Clark"

After dinner we went from the Club to the bus station and spent our last hour together there. My last hour with my little boy who grew up and became Corky's "My Daddy"! I like to think of him as he stood watching Corky trudge about the crowded waiting room. He was never far from the lad, but Corky thought that he was on his own. I saw him last, that final glimpse of his strong face, as he leaned across Betty and his son, smiling to me through the window; and then the bus was gone and it was dark, but the smile stays.

Clark's letters are something of him. The one that is the most beautiful gift he ever gave me was written after his ordination in New London. It shall be Corky's some day. That letter left me silent, humble, and in grateful tears. There is another letter, his very last letter to me, that has upon it the breath of the same high emotion in which he wrote even more fully to Betty. I shall speak of that letter a little later.

The day that Clark reached his port of embarkation he wrote Betty this letter: "Dearest: I can't write a 'noble, brave' letter.

I would be a little self-conscious writing that sort of a letter to you. All that I can say is that always I will love you and hold our happy memories in the most sacred part of my thoughts until that time when we shall be together again. . . ."

And then in his last letter to Betty, the one that came after his ship had steamed away into the danger-crowded waters of the North Atlantic, he wrote: "There is a part of my mind that is quite satisfied with the turn of events that sends me to the safe but lonely post we have talked about. However, you know there is another part of me that is disappointed. Perhaps all of us are drawn to the heroic and hazardous. I have done all and more than is legitimate to get into the thick of it. . . . Dearest, I love you, and wherever I go and for all time I am yours, and you are mine. Read to Corky for me and spank him, love him, keep him away from the river, and feed him the oil! You must let me know how things are with 'Thumper' and send me a wire. . . . God bless you, my darling wife. . . ."

Thumper is with us now—Corky's lovely sister Susan Elizabeth. Clark, remembering the little rabbit in Bambi, gave her the name "Thumper," and quite appropriate it was! He went away dreaming happy dreams of the little son or daughter who presently would be in Betty's arms awaiting his return. And it was so soon—so very soon after Baby Susan arrived that another great sorrow came to Corky's mother. Her own lovely mother was suddenly taken from her. Clark had said to Corky's grandmother, "You'll take care of Betty for me, won't you, Mother? You'll be with her when Thumper comes." And it seemed that in spite of her steadily growing suffering and weakness, she lived just to keep that promise.

Clark's dream was not to come true, though I am very sure it never faded from his sight. On the eleventh of February, 1943, Betty called from Schenectady and told our mother in Philadelphia that a telegram had come from the Adjutant General's Office in

Washington informing her that Clark was "missing in action" in the North Africa area. I was in Washington completing the details of an overseas mission when Betty telephoned, and I did not have the disturbing word until I came to the old house late in the evening. Then I reassured them all, because I knew that it was a mistake. Clark's ship could not have reached North African waters. There had not been time. And a mistake it proved to be—but a mistake that when corrected brought no reassurance, for the correction read "North Atlantic." It was very hard to fly away leaving all whom I loved with "missing in action" ever before their eyes.

I flew the Atlantic, came to Horta in the Azores and to Lisbon in Portugal and on to London, hoping for a message, praying for a better word, but knowing always that war is no respecter of families and that one who has preached to others should above all others practice what he has preached. Yes, and knowing, too, that Clark would expect all of us to be good soldiers.

Clark was that, a good soldier. Even now we know little about the tragic night when the cargo-transport ship *Dorchester* was torpedoed off the coast of Greenland and sank within a few short miles of her destination and so close to safety. I have talked to only two of those who were with him on that ship and who knew him. But we do know that with three other chaplains who were his comrades and friends, he was true to his high calling, true to the finest traditions of the chaplaincy, and that he completed his mission. The story as we knew it then was written for the service in Baptist Temple, when after my return from Europe and Africa in April, 1943, we dedicated the flag I had carried back from City Temple, London. Governor Edward Martin of Pennsylvania spoke the message of dedication and these are the words written about Clark and his fellow chaplains:

CLARK VANDERSALL POLING

On February 13, the War Department reported to his wife, Elizabeth Jung Poling, Chaplain Clark Poling, second son of Dr. and Mrs. Poling, "missing in action in the North African area." Later, the location was corrected to "North Atlantic area," and on Monday, April 10, "missing in action" was officially changed to "lost in action." While full particulars have not been released, Chaplain Poling was one of four chaplains in three faiths who were on the cargo transport *Dorchester*, which sank in iceberg waters within twenty-five minutes after being torpedoed at 1:15 A.M. February 3. At that time, the ship was within ninety miles of its Greenland destination. Of the 904 men on board, 678 are reported "lost in action."

In the affidavit filed by Frank A. Benkler, Quartermaster, Merchant Marine Service, and signed by Fred Francis Bibler (Night Steward) and Juan L. Alejandro (Gun Crew Messman), appears the following: "The following incident was told by soldier survivors to crew survivors. Authenticity can be verified by the soldier survivors now in Greenland concerning the heroic conduct of the four chaplains aboard the sinking ship—Jewish, Catholic, Protestant. With utter disregard of self, having given away their life-jackets to four men without them, the chaplains stood hand in hand, praying to God they served for the safety of those men who were leaving the stricken ship on all sides of them. This is the picture engraved on our minds and hearts as the ship disappeared beneath the waves." The complete affidavit is filed in the Office of the Chief of Chaplains, Washington, D. C.

More recently Dr. Poling has talked with another survivor, Engineer Grady Clark, who is convalescing in an Army hospital from frozen limbs and shock. Just before slipping over the side of the ship, he stood within "eight feet of Chaplain Poling." Having obeyed orders, Grady was fully clothed and in his life-jacket, so that, after nearly nine hours in the water, he was rescued—perhaps then the only remaining survivor. He confirms the above report, and adds, "They quieted the panic, forced the men 'frozen' on the rail toward the boats or over the side, helped men adjust life-jackets, and at last gave away their own. They themselves had no chance without life-jackets." He spoke of Chaplain Poling's contagious laugh, and concluded, "I swam away from the ship and turned to watch. The flares now lighted everything. The bow came up high and she slid under. The last I saw, the chaplains were up there praying for the safety of the men. They had done everything they could. I did not see them again."

Alexander D. Goode, the Jew; Father John P. Washington, the Catholic; George L. Fox and Clark Poling, the Protestants. Four men in three faiths, joined in friendship and sharing in a holy mission, in death were not divided. Lost in action, they were found of God.

Significant of the brief life and ministry of Clark Poling are these words from his last letter to me: "Apparently I am headed for a blind alley, but, Dad, if when I get there I find one other man, then there will be three of us." That letter reminded me of what Clark once wrote from prep-school after he had listened to an address delivered by a great-hearted missionary from the Sudan country in Africa. It was his first expression of the kind, the first of his religious statements: "Now I know that I could follow Jesus to the death," he said. In the material from Dean Weigle's file which I have included in the Postscript appears this sentence from a letter written by a professor of Hope College: "He wants action of an heroic sort—though not mock heroic." Dr. Weigle has said of these comments: "The fact that they were written eleven years ago, in answer to our inquiry about him while he was still a senior in college, gives them all the more value."

It was in a hotel just off Grosvenor Square in London that the final word reached me—though even then I would not give it my final acceptance—the word that "missing in action" must reasonably be changed to "lost in action." The radio blared the story of the transport torpedoed and of survivors picked up, "frozen at the oars"; of panic on the deck, of less than twenty-five minutes between the time of the explosion and the rising of the bow high in the air as the stricken ship slid under. But chiefly the announcer spoke of four chaplains of three faiths who did their bit, gave their life-belts to enlisted men and then in prayer together went down with the ship.

In my room I sat with my thoughts—my thoughts of Clark and of Corky, of Thumper and of Betty. They were long thoughts that reached back across the years and that traveled down the world. All those I loved were in them, and the Long House with the dreams of a little boy. That night I had a dream, a dream of Wolf Hill renamed. I said in my dream, "It shall be Clark's Summit now, and there shall be a memorial there, simple but worthy, to each of the chaplains, and a flag always flying, and the granite mountain shall become an inter-faith shrine, and in the peace it shall tell men that beyond all else there is a unity that transcends their differences of faith and race." That dream is coming true.

Perhaps then I dozed, but also I remembered a letter, another letter, Clark's first letter to me. It was written when he was seven, written in square, block letters and addressed by his mother to me in France. It reached me on the first Friday of February, 1918, found me in a dugout of Rambecourt, on the Toul Sector of the Western Front of another world war. That letter reads: "Dear Daddy: Gee, I wish I was where you are. Love, Clark." And it had come to pass that in exactly twenty-five years after the "war to end war," the war "to make the world safe for Democracy," had been fought and won, the desire of an eager little boy had been granted.

Morning came at last and I went to Cheltenham, the famous English Spa. "SOS," it was then. I had been scheduled there for a week end of speaking engagements. Cheltenham, you will remember, is the city where in 1926 we found Joan. I was glad to be busy.

On Monday night I returned to London, bound for the great bomber stations. I was the guest of Lieutenant General Lee on his military train, and had the compartment next to his. We retired late; but as I sat on my bed, the senior chaplain, Father Ternan, knocked and came in. Matters of this character are not discussed in the Service, but always there is an understanding silence; where death is for so many constantly so near, words are seldom needed or timely. But now the great-hearted chaplain sat by my side, dropped his hand on my knee, and said, "I shall pray for you at the Mass in the morning and for his wife and son and for his mother." He was silent, and then he added, "It will comfort you to remember that God also gave His son." Then he went out.

Something akin to that in its impression on me was a paragraph from a letter written by Clark's sister Rachel: "I shall always remember Clark as he was at the age of my own little son "Dutch," remember him as a shy but affectionate little brother. We were at Sagamore Beach on Cape Cod and when he wasn't digging clams or playing in the surf, his nose was in a book. I think so much of him now and of all the others who are giving their lives that Corky and Dutch and all other children shall not grow up to fight another war. How I pray that his sacrifice and theirs has not been in vain."

I was up at three A.M. and shaving, ready to hurry across the city to another station to catch my train for the Midlands, when Lieutenant General John C. H. Lee came in. A great military leader, equally great he is as a Christian. He learned that I used the same book of daily devotional readings that he read. After the early breakfast, he stepped with me to the car which waited at the vestibule door. He stood looking at me, stood quietly, looking intently. Then he saluted and said, "Sir, there would be, I think, one thing harder for you than giving a son—not having had a son to give."

That was all, but I was comforted and the night became as the day. Yes, in such a time as this one should be glad to live and, if need be, die. And for a cause such as Clark's, one should be sadly proud to give a son.

Nor do we ever think of his life as ended, for we know that he is marching still and that he has only "finished to begin." He believed that this life so dear and wonderful to us is but the childhood of our immortality, and though he planned and hoped to return—planned and hoped with a passionate hunger for Betty and Corky and Thumper—his was the Christian's immortal hope. . . . He will be waiting for us just around the corner. Surely, as another has said, "He took Heaven with the wind in his face."

Clark's sister Jane wrote me a very wonderful letter on Father's Day after the *Dorchester* went down. In it she said: "We are so fortunate, Daddy. We have no coffin and no wasted body. No lonely grave and no dismal cemetery. We have the broad Atlantic, and the Atlantic in all its moods is like Clark."

I dreamed about Clark one night as I slept in my berth riding from London to Glasgow. It was a strange but somewhat comforting dream, a dream in which we talked together about little children, and of course Corky was in the dream.

Later I sat in my room and wrote these verses, my tribute to a memory, the memory of Corky's "My Daddy," and let them be my humble tribute to all those youthful, radiant lives who have given, and yet will give, that "last full measure" that freedom and justice, Christian mercy and the hope of man's brotherhood in God's fatherhood, shall not be destroyed.

VALIANTLY AND SOON

They keep their rendezvous with death,
 So valiantly and soon:
They pledge their youth and give their all
 "And rest before their noon."

Now God will give them greater things,
 And have them by His side;
And rested they shall build new worlds
 Where death itself has died.

A LETTER TO SUSAN

Dear Susan:

You were "Thumper" to your daddy—he gave you the little rabbit's name from BAMBI. *And it is of Thumper he is thinking, along with your brother, in his last letter to your mother. He never saw you, but you were in his dreams, I know; and perhaps, my dear, as you were coming in and he was going out your spirits met as ships that pass in the night. Perhaps he heard—yes, Susan, I am sure he did—heard your first cry and was glad.*

For such as he there is no death, no end of knowing. Absent he is, but not away; and you shall have him through the years till Time and Space shall meet the great Forever and you shall know each other there.

POSTSCRIPT

AN ANSWER TO A QUESTION

How can I know God?

"Through Jesus Christ! and, of course, through prayer, Bible study, and service to men, women, and children. God is a Being so great and so good that when we are rightly related to Him, we are spiritually prepared for whatever experience we have to meet."

The man who wrote that demonstrated its truth.

CLARK POLING AS I KNEW HIM

By Ernest M. Ligon *

Let me tell you about Clark Poling as I knew and loved him, scolded and congratulated him, was angered and inspired by him.

I suppose he made as many personal friends during his short ministry here as anyone ever did. His gift for attracting people to himself was astonishing. I introduced him to many people when he first came; he introduced me to many more before he left.

It is not easy to put into words the charm of his personality, because its most characteristic qualities defy description. And yet it was so unique that no one would ever confuse him with anyone else. His very weaknesses served only to bring his personal magnetism into focus. You must know them if you are to know Clark.

You had to sit two hours beyond the appointed time, waiting for him to appear for a dinner appointment, knowing that the dinner would be ruined—and then have him appear another time unexpectedly with a huge steak and all the fixings in his hands; you had to go to a meeting he had scheduled only to find him absent because he had scheduled two others at the same time someplace else—and then watch him by sheer force of sincerity persuade a church board to vote unanimously for something they did not understand and which they could see no way of financing; you had to see him lock himself in his study on a Sunday morning at nine to prepare a sermon to be delivered at ten-thirty, which then

* Associate Professor of Psychology, Union College. Consultant in Character Education, First Reformed Church, Schenectady, N. Y.

lasted fifteen minutes longer than usual—and then see him at a dinner rise to such speaking heights as to outdo completely the guest of honor, his illustrious father. His sincerity was complete and caused great force. His almost naïve frankness made him say things from the pulpit that on occasion left his hearers shocked, amused, aghast, or inspired. He was the most irresponsible responsible person and the most disorganized successful organizer I ever knew.

I have known him to misplace a birth or wedding certificate, only to find it among his income tax papers. When our phone rang after midnight, we assumed that it would be Clark. He never went home before 2 A.M. But when he decided to get his church to participate in the Union-Westminster Character Research Project, he personally described it individually to every member of his congregation. He must have spent hundreds of hours at that job. As a result he had a completely united church when the venture was officially launched.

I have been so angry at him that I was ready to chew nails, only to have that infectious grin of his melt my ire in the twinkling of an eye. I suppose that grin, plus his complete and unquestioned sincerity, more than anything else was responsible for his power.

Clark came to Schenectady and in five years transformed a church that was virtually dead into one that was fast becoming the most influential in the community. And in his death left so great an influence that his church has not hesitated to set forth on a highly ambitious church school project as a memorial. Even in his death he is intensely alive.

He did a good job of choosing a wife. Betty's personality and charm are quite on a par with his. She gave much to him and undoubtedly gained much from him, which will greatly broaden her sympathy and understanding for whatever responsibilities life imposes upon her. His son seems to be the spittin' image of his father in dynamic energy that runs amuck more often than not, and in personal charm that conquers all before it.

Personally, I owe much to Clark. He threw in his lot with the Character Research Project the second year he was here. It might never have had an opportunity but for the vision and tenacity of Clark. I do not know how long people will remember the name, Clark Poling, but in the character education of the future, he will live in influence and power.

This is certainly an inadequate picture of Clark, but I think you will agree that here was a Christian personality—dynamically Christian and I do mean "Personality. . . ."

DEAN WEIGLE'S LETTER

Reverend Daniel A. Poling
The Baptist Temple
Broad and Berks Streets
Philadelphia, Pa.
Dear Dan:

. . . I have been looking over Clark's folder here and I want to send you quotations from what was written about him when he made application to enter this school back in 1933.

From Hope College: "His record here was good; he was a leader in several extra-curricular activities, always exerted the best influence among his mates, and demonstrated a well-poised, strong manhood. A bit impulsive at times, he found that he had to retrace steps occasionally; but the impulse was always along lines calculated to bring good. This impulse will doubtless develop into initiative—of which we need plenty today! I am certain that he will make an outstanding worker in Christian service, and I should regret his entrance into any other type of work."

From Hope College: "Mr. Clark Poling, who is applying to you for admission, is an interesting person. He is candid and very courageous concerning what he believes to be true. He has a persistent belief, too, that there is truth beyond physical facts, though he never defies facts that are important.

"He used to defy English orthography in my rhetoric and literature classes, where he wrote some of the best themes and reports I have ever received. This seemed bad to me, but he would not be concerned about the matter. He has considerable social grace and a great deal of spontaneity in speaking and writing. He despises sham. As a student he is good, but not a scholar. He wants action of an heroic sort, though not mock-heroic.

"If he comes to Yale, I think both Yale and Poling are to be congratulated."

From Rutgers University: "Clark Poling is a man of real promise of usefulness in the Christian ministry, as evidenced through excellent scholastic work and a fine personality. His character has been above reproach, and he has been a leader among his fellow students in a quiet and efficient manner. I believe that Clark Poling will become a leader in the ministry. I consider him a type that is most needed in that field."

From Rutgers University: "Of no other student I have known during my seven years at Rutgers University could I speak with the same lack of mental reservation. With an enthusiastic idealism, a hearty friendliness, a keen mind, and a cultured urbanity, I believe that he is exceptionally well fitted, both by natural ability and by careful training, to profit by the training he will be able to get in your school. I find it hard to speak of Mr. Poling without seeming to be uncritically eulogistic."

From Oakwood School: "While Clark was in school, he was noted for having strong convictions to which he was very loyal. He would stand up against the whole faculty at one time and at another against the majority of the student body. He would do all of these in a very nice way. He was the most influential student in his class. It is difficult for me to speak with moderation of Clark Poling. He is one of the most attractive students we have had in Oakwood School and has great promise in the Christian ministry. He is fundamentally honest; he not only tells the truth, he makes every possible effort to know the truth. He is a hard worker. He has a contagious enthusiasm and a fine sense of humor. I expect him to be an even greater man than his father."

These letters were sent us in confidence, but I am sure that th writers would be willing to have me quote them in this way There is no reservation at any point accompanying any of thes letters. The fact that they were written eleven years ago in answe to our inquiry about him while he was still a senior in college give them all the more value.

As for my own contact with Clark, I just want to say that he made upon me the impression that he had already made upon hi teachers in school and college. It is my privilege, as you know, to deal, year after year, with a highly selected group of young mer who are in training here for the Christian ministry—men o preparation for the Christian ministry which Yale University affords them. We do not get many weaklings and we get a great many young men of real strength. I know of no one among these students of whose all-around fitness for the Christian ministry I have felt more sure than I was sure with respect to Clark. His initiative was tempered with a high sense of responsibility and his spontaneity with unusual regard for others. He had the impulsiveness of a great soul, yet he was dependable to the last bit of what the situation required.

I count it a great joy, Dan, to have had him as one of my pupils and to have shared in his ordination.

With warm regard,

Sincerely yours,

Luther

Dr. Luther A. Weigle, Dean
Yale Divinity School
New Haven, Conn.